The
Working Mother
Cookbook

• • •

ALSO FROM THE EDITORS OF *Working Mother*

•   •   •

The Working Mother *Book of Time*

The
Working Mother
Cookbook

Fast, Easy Recipes from

Working Mother magazine

• • •

Susan Lilly Ott, Food Editor

ST. MARTIN'S GRIFFIN ⚩ NEW YORK

www.stmartins.com

Library of Congress Cataloging-in-Publication Data

The Working mother cookbook : fast, easy recipes from the editors of Working mother mgazine.—1st ed.
    p.   cm.
1. Quick and easy cookery.   2. Menus.   I. Working mother (New York, N.Y. : 1981)
TX833.5. W67 2000
641.5'55—dc21   00-031769

ISBN 0-312-26698-7

First Edition: October 2000

10   9   8   7   6   5   4   3   2   1

Contents

7-Day Dinner Plans

Desserts: Sweet and Simple

Introduction

Dear Reader,

Families that eat dinner together have a shared time for both connection and conversation that can help strengthen their bonds and ease the tensions of the day. But that can only happen if getting food to the table is as hassle-free as possible. For working moms that means meals that are quick to prepare and are tasty and appealing to kids and adults alike.

Our hope is that you will use the recipe plans in this book as a guide so you can find the best way for you and your family to handle dinnertime together. This cookbook should bring pleasure and ease to your life—use it as a guide, not a scheduler. The last thing we want to do is make you feel like you have to make a family meal *every* night to be a "good" mother. Most supermarkets now carry excellent and affordable prepared foods. Make the most of them. Find which foods your family likes best, and add them to your weekly shopping list. A simple rotisserie chicken waiting for you in the refrigerator means all you have to do is cook a pot of rice and toss a salad. I know a family that religiously has take-out pizza every Friday night; it's a family celebration that everyone looks forward to all week—not a last-minute attempt to get food, any food, on the table.

At the end of the day, the most important thing is for the family to reconnect. We hope our recipes and meal plans will help you enjoy doing just that around your dinner table. That is what we, at *Working Mother* magazine, are all about. Families being together as much as possible, learning from each other, sharing fun . . . and food.

Lisa Benenson
Editor-in-Chief, *Working Mother*

How This Cookbook Works

No matter what the ingredients or the flavors, the cuisine or cooking style, all our recipes offer great flavors, good basic nutrition, and ease of preparation.

Over and over, through surveys *Working Mother* has conducted, you have told us that you want a wide range of tastes and food styles to choose from. Sometimes you want meat-and-potatoes-style meals; other times pastas, grains, and salads suit your mood. Sometimes you're in the mood for family favorites; other times you like to experiment with exotic flavors and new ingredients. But one thing all working moms always want is simplicity.

Throughout this book you'll find the most remarkably flavorful meals that are a breeze to get on the table. Whether you use our quick-fix 29-Minute Meal plans, our cook-now-eat-later Freeze-Ahead system, or the wonderfully organized 7-Day Dinner Plans, you'll discover that creating an enjoyable, healthful family mealtime is possible even on busy weeknights.

Another plus is that the recipes are quite generous—when they say they serve four, you're likely to have leftovers. And that means you'll have great food on hand for pick-up dinners or lunches.

29-Minute Meals

These menus present complete meals that take less than a half hour to prepare. The recipes are streamlined and straightforward, with just a few steps. They use a minimum of cooking utensils, thereby cutting down on cleanup time. They also make good use of the many convenience products now available that help keep preparation and cooking times to a minimum without sacrificing flavor.

Freeze-Ahead Meals

Our Freeze-Ahead Recipes are a boon to moms who prefer to spend a little extra time in the kitchen over the weekend, then forget about cooking for a week or so. We offer Big Batch Recipes that make multiple meals and Master Recipes that can be used to create a variety of dishes.

7-Day Dinner Plans

This clever cooking strategy does all the planning and organizing for you. You take the provided shopping list to the market and then follow the recipes. Choose from seven dinner plans, each one a week's worth of speedy, weeknight meals made from extra food cooked on the weekend. And check out the Holiday Plan to make Thanksgiving or other major feasts—and the week after—easier to organize, execute, and recover from!

Sweet Treats: Desserts You Can Do . . . Tonight

The dessert recipes offered here are designed to give you an occasional break from ice cream and cookies, without taking a lot of time or effort.

29-Minute Meals

• • •

Ground Rules for Preparing 29-Minute Meals

- *Read through the entire recipe before beginning.* Note the game plan outlined in the introduction to each recipe. It provides a schedule.

- *Take care of getting one item ready while another item is cooking.* Use the time while the broiler heats and pasta water comes to a boil to prep the meat and chop the vegetables. While the sauce simmers or meat cooks, set the table or toss the salad. (It's a busy, but amazingly productive, half hour).

- *Reuse bowls and pots to minimize cleanup.* If a skillet is needed to cook two ingredients or recipes, wipe out the skillet with a paper towel after the first use and then reuse.

- *Cook things together.* If you're making a pasta and broccoli dish, why not add the broccoli to the boiling pasta and save on cleanup? How about warming the bread in the oven while the meat broils?

- *Don't avoid convenience products available at your market.* And think about using those products for more than their stated purpose. Precut salad-bar vegetables are perfect for a stir-fry. Refrigerated biscuits make great individualized pizzas for the kids. Some of the products you can depend on and we can't live without: packaged salad mixes, prepared salad dressing, canned chicken stock, canned beans, ready-made refrigerated pizza dough and biscuits, grated cheeses, bottled pasta sauces, seasoned rice mixes, and ready-cut fresh vegetables, like broccoli and carrots.

Seared Basil Sea Scallops with Emerald Orzo and Fresh Tomato Salad

SHOPPING TIP

There are two types of scallops: sea scallops, used here, which are about 1½ inches in diameter, and tiny bay scallops (about ½ inch in diameter), which are rarer, sweeter, and more expensive. Buy the larger, meatier sea scallops for this dish. Scallops should be refrigerated as soon as possible, and should be cooked within 2 days of purchase. Like all shellfish, scallops cook very quickly, and will toughen if overcooked.

GAME PLAN

1. Put water for orzo on to boil. Warm oil in skillet.

2. Stuff the scallops.

3. Slice thinly 2 large beefsteak tomatoes and arrange on a platter.

4. When water boils, add orzo. While it cooks, quick-cook the scallops. Drizzle the tomatoes with a prepared salad dressing from the refrigerator.

5. Assemble platter with orzo and scallops. Bring it and platter of tomatoes to table and serve.

Seared Basil Scallops

Although they're expensive, scallops are worth the price. The flavor is delicate; there's nothing to shell, clean, or fillet—and they cook in the blink of an eye.

1 lb large sea scallops (about 24)
2 T refrigerated prepared pesto
2 T olive oil
¼ cup fresh lemon juice (from about 2 lemons)

1. For each scallop: Using a sharp knife, cut most, but not all, of the way through the side of each scallop, so you make a small pocket.

2. Spread about ¼ tsp of the pesto in the pocket; close scallop.

3. Warm olive oil in large nonstick skillet over high heat. Add scallops; brown for 2 minutes on each side, until cooked through. Remove to warm plate.

4. Turn off heat under skillet, add lemon juice, and cook about 10 seconds, stirring to incorporate browned bits. Pour pan juices over scallops. Keep warm until orzo is done.

Emerald Orzo

1. Cook 1 cup orzo according to package directions; drain.

2. In medium serving bowl, toss cooked orzo with ⅓ cup refrigerated prepared pesto. (Use more or less as you desire.)

3. Place orzo on platter, arrange scallops on top.

SERVES 4

Nutritional Information

PER SERVING OF SCALLOPS: 201 cal, 18 g protein, 12 g fat, 5 g carbohydrate, 36 mg cholesterol, 495 mg sodium
PER SERVING OF ORZO: 221 cal, 7 g protein, 10 g fat, 26 g carbohydrate, 8 mg cholesterol, 302 mg sodium

KITCHEN TIP

*Peel fresh ginger
with a paring knife
or vegetable peeler,
then put a small
chunk into a garlic
press and squeeze.
Peeled fresh ginger
will keep, if tightly
wrapped, in your re-
frigerator for up to 3
weeks.*

We like this vibrant main-dish salad with plain white rice, but feel free to substitute a packaged seasoned rice mix.

 GAME PLAN

1. Start cooking the rice, then make the salad dressing and marinate the chicken.

2. Prep vegetables for the stir-fry while the chicken cooks.

Slaw and Chicken

1 lb boneless, skinless chicken tenders, cut into 1-in chunks
1 tsp salt
1 bag (16 oz) sliced cabbage or coleslaw mix
3 scallions, thinly sliced
8 oz snow peas, trimmed
1 medium red pepper, thinly sliced
⅓ cup salted roasted peanuts

1. In mixing bowl, toss chicken chunks with 2 T of the dressing (see recipe below) and salt.

2. In large nonstick skillet over medium-high heat, cook chicken 6 minutes, stirring.

3. In large serving bowl, combine cabbage and scallions.

4. Add snow peas, red pepper, and 2 T of the dressing to cooking chicken; sauté 2 minutes.

5. Remove skillet from heat; toss chicken and vegetables in serving bowl with cabbage mixture, along with remaining dressing. Garnish with peanuts. Serve on rice.

Dressing

6 T canola oil
¼ cup rice vinegar
2 T Asian sesame oil
1 T peeled, minced fresh ginger
2 tsp reduced-sodium soy sauce

In medium bowl, whisk ingredients until blended.

Warm White Rice

1. In medium saucepan over high heat, combine 1cup long-grain white rice, ½ tsp salt, and 2 cups water.

2. Bring to a boil; reduce heat, cover and simmer about 19 minutes, until water has been absorbed.

SERVES **4**

Nutritional Information

PER SERVING OF ASIAN SLAW WITH SESAME CHICKEN: 519 cal, 33 g protein, 37 g fat, 15 g carbohydrate, 72 mg cholesterol, 791 mg sodium
PER SERVING OF RICE: 134 cal, 3 g protein, trace g fat, 29 g carbohydrate, 0 mg cholesterol, 267 mg sodium

SHOPPING TIP

*For easy stuffing,
select large chicken
breasts—each breast
half should weigh at
least 6 ounces. Be
sure to use the soft
white goat-cheese log,
not the natural log
with a brownish
rind.*

 GAME PLAN

1. Prep beans.

2. Make cheese stuffing and fill the chicken breasts.

3. Cook vegetables while the chicken simmers.

Goat-Cheese Stuffed Chicken Breasts

1 log (4 oz) soft goat cheese
1 clove garlic, halved
2 T fresh lemon juice (from 1 large lemon)
1 T chopped fresh tarragon or 1 tsp dried
¼ tsp black pepper
4 boneless, skinless chicken-breast halves (about 6 oz each)
2 T olive oil
¾ cup dry white wine

1. In food processor fitted with metal blade or blender, process first 5 ingredients. (They can be mixed by hand, but garlic should be minced.)

2. Using a sharp knife, cut a horizontal slit through thickest portion of each breast to form a deep pocket.

3. Stuff each pocket with an equal amount of cheese mixture; press edges together to seal.

4. Warm oil in large skillet over medium-high heat; brown breasts for 3 minutes on each side.

5. Reduce heat; add wine and cover. Simmer about 6 minutes, until chicken is cooked through.

6. Remove chicken to platter.

7. Increase heat under skillet to high; simmer liquid until slightly reduced.

8. Serve chicken drizzled with pan juices.

Glazed Baby Carrots and Beans

1. Warm 1 tsp olive oil in large skillet over medium-high heat.

2. Trim and halve ½ lb fresh green beans; peel ½ lb baby carrots.

3. Place beans and carrots in skillet. Add ¼ cup water.

4. Cook 4 minutes, stirring occasionally. Then stir in salt and black pepper to taste; cover and cook 4 minutes longer, or until vegetables are just tender-crisp. If desired, sprinkle with 1 T chopped fresh tarragon.

SERVES 4

Nutritional Information

PER SERVING OF CHICKEN: 309 cal, 32 g protein, 16 g fat, 1 g carbohydrate, 86 mg cholesterol, 170 mg sodium

PER SERVING OF CARROTS AND BEANS: 53 cal, 2 g protein, 1 g fat, 10 g carbohydrate, 0 mg cholesterol, 41 mg sodium

GAME PLAN

Start potatoes cooking and preheat grill, then form burgers.

Bull's-eye Burgers

3 lb lean ground beef
1 small onion, chopped
1 T Worcestershire sauce
1 T ketchup
1 tsp salt
½ tsp black pepper
½ lb sharp cheddar cheese, divided into 6 chunks
6 hamburger buns

1. In large bowl, combine first 6 ingredients.

2. Divide mixture into 6 portions, lightly shape each portion into a big ½-inch-thick patty.

3. Remove some of the meat from the top center of each patty; insert a chunk of cheese (flatten chunk slightly with your palm to fit in the hole). Replace meat over cheese.

4. Preheat grill to medium heat. Grill burgers for 5 to 7 minutes per side. If desired, toast buns by placing them, split-side down, on the edges of grill for about 1 minute.

Mashed Potato Salad

3 lb russet potatoes (about 6 large)
½ cup reduced-fat sour cream or
lowfat yogurt
¾ tsp salt

DRESSING:
½ cup olive oil   *¼ tsp black pepper*
2 T cider vinegar   *6 scallions, diced*
½ tsp salt   *¼ cup chopped fresh Italian parsley*

1. Peel potatoes and cut into 1-inch chunks.

2. Place in large saucepan; cover with salted warm water. Cover pan; bring to a boil and cook about 10 minutes, or until tender.

3. Drain; return potatoes to pan and cook over medium heat 30 seconds, or until excess liquid evaporates, shaking pan.

4. Remove from heat; stir in ½ cup reduced-fat sour cream or plain lowfat yogurt and ¾ tsp salt. While still hot, mash with a potato masher.

5. Combine dressing ingredients in jar with tight-fitting lid. Shake well.

6. Stir vinaigrette into potatoes, along with scallions and parsley. Serve hot or at room temparature.

SERVES **6**

Nutritional Information

PER SERVING OF HAMBURGER: 709 cal, 56 g protein, 42 g fat, 25 g carbohydrate, 193 mg cholesterol, 1000 mg sodium
PER SERVING OF POTATOES: 333 cal, 5 g protein, 17 g fat, 42 g carbohydrate, 3 mg cholesterol, 425 mg sodium

SHOPPING TIP

Unsweetened coconut milk is a combination of water and coconut meat that has been simmered and strained. It is available in the ethnic section of most supermarkets, as is Thai fish sauce.

 GAME PLAN

1. Preheat broiler, then get rice cooking.

2. Prepare lime marinade, and chop cilantro and scallions while the chicken marinates.

Thai Lime Chicken

2 large limes
½ tsp salt
2 boneless, skinless chicken breasts, cut in half
½ cup canned unsweetened coconut milk
¼ tsp cayenne pepper
1 tsp Thai fish sauce
2 scallions, thinly sliced

1. Preheat broiler.

2. From limes, grate 1¼ tsp peel, and squeeze ⅓ cup juice. Place 3 T of lime juice and ½ tsp salt in medium bowl. Marinate chicken in mixture for 5 minutes.

3. Line baking sheet with foil; place chicken breasts, smooth-side up. Broil 6 minutes. Flip breasts; broil 2 minutes longer or until cooked through. Transfer to serving platter.

4. While chicken is cooking, warm coconut milk, cayenne, and lime peel in saucepan over low heat. Remove from heat, stir in fish sauce and remaining 3 T lime juice.

5. To serve: Spoon ¼ cup of the coconut sauce over chicken on platter; garnish with scallions. Reserve remaining sauce for rice.

Zest

If a recipe calls for both the peel (or zest) and the juice of a citrus fruit, always remove the zest first, then juice the fruit. Use a citrus zester, a tool with tiny cutting holes at one end, that removes long, thin strands of peel, or a box grater. It's a good idea to go ahead and juice the whole fruit; refrigerate any unused juice in an airtight container, where it will keep for 5 days. Fresh citrus juice will add spark to almost any salad, fish, or vegetable. •

Coconut-Almond Pilaf

1 box (about 6 oz) almond rice pilaf
¼ cup chopped fresh cilantro or Italian parsley
¼ cup coconut sauce

1. Prepare 1 box almond rice pilaf according to package directions.

2. In medium serving bowl, toss hot rice with cilantro or Italian parsley and the coconut sauce.

SERVES **4**

Nutritional Information

PER SERVING OF CHICKEN: 198 cal, 27 g protein, 9 g fat, 1 g carbohydrate, 73 mg cholesterol, 336 mg sodium
PER SERVING OF PILAF: 72 cal, 1 g protein, 4 g fat, 9 g carbohydrate, 0 mg cholesterol, 164 mg sodium

To save time, ask the butcher to slice the pork for you.

GAME PLAN

1. While pork cooks, make the dressing and combine the bean mixture.

2. Toss the spinach salad just before serving.

Sautéed Pork Medallions and 3-Bean Medley

The same dressing is used to flavor both the bean medley and the spinach salad.

6 T olive oil
1¼ lb boneless pork tenderloin, cut into
 ¾-inch-thick medallions
1½ tsp salt
½ tsp black pepper
2 T balsamic vinegar
1 tsp Dijon mustard
1 medium shallot, chopped

1 can (15 oz) black beans, rinsed and
 drained
1 can (15 oz) kidney beans, rinsed and
 drained
1 can (15 oz) cannellini or white
 kidney beans, rinsed and drained
2 stalks celery, diced
3 T fresh Italian parsley, chopped

1. Preheat oven to 350°F. Warm 1 T of the oil in large ovenproof skillet over high heat.

2. Lay pork medallions out on a plate; sprinkle with 1 tsp of the salt and ¼ tsp of the pepper.

3. Set ½ of medallions in skillet so they are not touching. Cook about 2 minutes per side, until browned. Repeat with remaining pork.

4. When you have skillet-browned all the pork, return it all to the skillet. Place in oven and roast about 6 minutes, until just cooked through.

5. Meanwhile, in large serving bowl, combine vinegar, mustard, shallot, the remaining 5 T oil, ½ tsp of the salt, and ¼ tsp of the pepper. (Remove 2 T of the dressing; place in medium bowl. Set aside for use with spinach later.)

6. In large serving bowl, combine all beans, celery, and parsley with remaining dressing; toss to coat.

SHOPPING TIP

If baby spinach is unavailable, use regular spinach or any salad greens

Spinach Salad

1 bag (6–8 oz) fresh baby spinach
2 T reserved dressing

1. Trim spinach. Toss with dressing you've set aside in medium bowl.

2. Divide evenly on dinner plates; top with bean mixture. Place slices of pork along side.

SERVES **6**

Nutritional Information

PER SERVING OF PORK WITH BEANS: 325 cal, 31 g protein, 13 g fat, 26 g carbohydrate, 60 mg cholesterol, 896 mg sodium
PER SERVING OF SALAD: 29 cal, 1 g protein, 2 g fat, 1 g carbohydrate, 0 mg cholesterol, 61 mg sodium

SHOPPING TIP

You could also use 2 large (1 lb each) pre-baked pizza crusts (such as Boboli) and your oven for this meal. Just cover with toppings and bake according to package directions.

GAME PLAN

1. Prep the crusts, filling, and the salad ingredients while the grill preheats.

2. Drizzle the salad with dressing just before serving.

Grilled Sweet Corn and Black-Bean Pizza

4 ears fresh corn, cut from the cob (about 2 cups kernels), or 1 pkg (10 oz) frozen corn kernels
1 can (15 oz) black beans, drained and rinsed
4 oz (enough to fill 1 cup) shredded Monterey Jack cheese
1 large ripe tomato, diced
1 clove garlic, minced
1/4 tsp ground cumin
1/4 tsp black pepper
2 pkg (10- to 16-oz size) prepared pizza dough
2 T olive oil

1. Preheat grill to medium-high heat. In medium saucepan over high heat, bring about 1 inch of water to a boil. Add corn kernels and boil 1 minute; drain well.

2. In large bowl combine corn, beans, cheese, tomato, garlic, cumin, and pepper.

3. Divide dough into 4 equal pieces. On lightly floured board, press 1 piece of dough with your hands to form a 10-inch round, about 1/4-inch thick. Repeat process with remaining pieces.

4. With a brush or your fingers, spread oil over top of pizza rounds.

5. Flip 1 dough round onto grill, oil-side down. Grill 60 to 90 seconds, until bottom stiffens and turns golden. With tongs, quickly and carefully flip crust. Sprinkle 1/4 of corn mixture onto crust. Slide pizza to side of grill with cooler coals. Grill 3 minutes, or until cheese melts and topping is heated through. Repeat with remaining dough and toppings.

Retro Iceberg Salad

1 small head iceberg lettuce
2 tomatoes, quartered
Prepared blue-cheese dressing

Core lettuce; slice into quarters. Place each quarter on a serving plate. Add 2 pieces of tomato to each salad. Drizzle prepared blue-cheese salad dressing over lettuce wedge.

SERVES **4**

Nutritional Information

PER SERVING OF PIZZA: 660 cal, 26 g protein, 22 g fat, 94 g carbohydrate, 25 mg cholesterol, 1200 mg sodium
PER SERVING OF SALAD: 54 cal, 3 g protein, 3 g fat, 5 g carbohydrate, trace mg cholesterol, 381 mg sodium

COOKING TIP

We love grilling pizzas on hot summer nights. But be warned—the crusts cook so fast that you must quickly move them to the side of the grill after flipping.

GAME PLAN

1. Preheat the oven for the tortillas.

2. Get the potatoes cooking before you start the eggs.

Huevos Rancheros con Frijoles

Because each tortilla is assembled separately, you can omit any filling ingredients that your kids don't like.

4 large (10-inch size) flour tortillas
2 T unsalted butter
1 small onion, chopped
1 red pepper, finely chopped
4 large eggs
1 can (15 oz) red kidney beans,
*   drained and rinsed*

1 cup prepared chunky salsa, in desired
*   spiciness*
¼ tsp hot pepper sauce
¼ tsp salt
½ cup (2 oz) shredded cheddar cheese
Chopped fresh cilantro (optional)

1. Preheat oven to 200°F. Wrap tortillas in foil; place in oven to warm.

2. Melt butter in large skillet over medium heat. Cook onion and pepper 5 minutes, stirring frequently until softened.

3. Push vegetables to edges of skillet. Break eggs into center of skillet. Cook sunny-side up or over easy, as desired. Transfer warmed tortillas to serving plates and top each with an egg.

4. Add beans, salsa, hot sauce, and salt to vegetables remaining in the skillet and heat through, stirring constantly. Spoon mixture over eggs; top with cheese. Sprinkle with cilantro, if desired.

5. Fold over tortillas, or serve open faced.

Eggs without Guilt—Almost

For decades, we were led to believe that for otherwise healthy people eating eggs was a major contributor to heart disease. We're happy to report that recent studies indicate this is not the case. Research now shows that saturated fat (found in animal products), not dietary cholesterol, is responsible for elevated cholesterol levels. One egg has around 1.6 grams of saturated fat. •

Chili Hash Browns

1 pkg (1 lb) frozen hash browns
¼ tsp chili powder
Salt and pepper to taste

Cook hash browns according to package directions. Sprinkle with chili powder and salt and pepper to taste.

SERVES **4**

Nutritional Information

PER SERVING HUEVOS RANCHEROS CON FRIJOLES: 440 cal, 20 g protein, 20 g fat, 48 g carbohydrate, 242 mg cholesterol, 925 mg sodium
PER SERVING OF POTATOES: 185 cal, 3 g protein, 10 g fat, 24 g carbohydrate, 0 mg cholesterol, 30 mg sodium

SHOPPING TIP

Ask your butcher to pound the chicken breast halves to ¼-inch thickness. If you pound them yourself, place the breast between two pieces of plastic wrap, and pound lightly with a flat-bottomed pan.

 GAME PLAN

1. Preheat the broiler and put on water for pasta.

2. Coat and cook the chicken.

Chicken Tenders Parmesan

1 large egg
½ tsp salt
¾ cup dry bread crumbs
¼ tsp black pepper
1 large (16 oz each) boneless, skinless chicken breast cut in half (with tenders attached), pounded to ¼-inch-thick cutlets

¼ cup olive oil
½ cup grated part-skim mozzarella cheese
¼ cup grated Parmesan cheese

1. Preheat broiler. In pie plate or shallow bowl, whisk egg with ¼ tsp of salt until blended. In another plate, combine bread crumbs, the remaining ¼ tsp salt and pepper.

2. For each cutlet: Dip both sides in egg mixture, then in bread crumbs; set aside on large plate.

3. Warm oil in large skillet over medium-high heat. Cook cutlets 3 minutes on each side.

4. Remove from skillet and place on wire rack set over a baking pan. Top cutlets with equal portions of cheeses. Place baking pan in oven; broil 2 minutes, until cheese melts.

5. Remove from broiler and slice each cutlet in half. Serve with spaghetti and extra marinara sauce.

Spaghetti Marinara

8 oz spaghetti
1 cup prepared marinara sauce

1. Cook 8 oz spaghetti according to package directions; drain. In small saucepan over low heat, warm marinara sauce.

2. In medium bowl, toss ¾ cup of the sauce with pasta. Spoon remaining ¼ cup sauce over cutlets, as desired.

SERVES **4**

Nutritional Information

PER SERVING OF CHICKEN: 350 cal, 24 g protein, 22 g fat, 14 g carbohydrate, 102 mg cholesterol, 666 mg sodium
PER SERVING OF SPAGHETTI: 257 cal, 9 g protein, 3 g fat, 49 g carbohydrate, 0 mg cholesterol, 349 mg sodium

GAME PLAN

1. Preheat broiler and start water boiling for pasta.

2. Make the creamy ricotta sauce and trim the peas.

3. Broil the shrimp while the pasta cooks.

Three-Pea Creamy Pasta Salad

Make this luscious pasta salad in the early summer, when sugar snaps are in season.

¾ lb small shell or penne pasta
1 large lemon
1 container (15 oz) part-skim ricotta cheese
3 T extra-virgin olive oil
1½ tsp salt
½ tsp black pepper
6 oz small sugar-snap peas, trimmed
6 oz snow peas, trimmed
1 pkg (10 oz) tiny frozen peas, thawed
½ cup chopped fresh basil or Italian parsley

1. Cook pasta according to package directions.

2. From lemon, grate 2 tsp peel, and squeeze 3 T juice.

3. In food processor fitted with metal blade, process peel, juice, ricotta, oil, salt, and pepper until completely smooth.

Peas and Q's

How to prepare fresh snap and snow peas? They both need to be de-strung before eating. Grasp the blossom end and pull gently along the seam. (The string will come off in one long fiber.)

With practice, this is a task a school-age child can do. Fresh snow peas are available all year long, while fresh sugar snaps are around only in the spring and summer.

Frozen varieties are not recommended. •

---

4. Place all peas in large strainer set in sink. Drain pasta into strainer; the hot water will blanch peas. Return pasta-pea mixture to cooking pot.

5. Stir in 1 cup of the ricotta sauce along with basil. (You'll have some ricotta sauce left over, which will keep for about a week in the fridge.)

Skewered Shrimp

12 oz large shrimp, shelled and deveined
olive oil
salt

1. Preheat broiler. Divide shrimp onto 6 skewers (you should have 4 to 6 shrimp on each skewer). Brush shrimp with 1 T olive oil and sprinkle with ¼ tsp salt.

2. Broil about 3 minutes, turning once, until just pink. Serve with pasta salad.

SERVES 6

Nutritional Information

PER SERVING OF PASTA SALAD: 289 cal, 15 g protein, 11 g fat, 33 g carbohydrate, 19 mg cholesterol, 405 mg sodium
PER SERVING OF SHRIMP: 67 cal, 12 g protein, 2 g fat, trace g carbohydrate, 86 mg cholesterol, 173 mg sodium

SHOPPING TIP

Our version of this famous French main-dish salad uses fresh tuna, but feel free to substitute canned— just drain and toss with 2 T of the dressing before serving.

GAME PLAN

1. Preheat oven to warm rolls, and start water boiling for the potatoes.

2. Make the dressing and marinate the fish.

3. While the potatoes cook, trim the beans, then cook the tuna.

Fresh Tuna Salad Niçoise

12 oz small red new potatoes (about 8), unpeeled and halved
¼ cup olive oil
3 T tarragon or white-wine vinegar
2 T drained capers, optional
1 T chopped fresh tarragon
2 tsp Dijon mustard
1 tsp anchovy paste, optional

1 clove garlic, minced
1 lb fresh tuna steaks, about 1 inch thick
½ lb fresh green beans, trimmed
1 bag (10 oz) salad greens
½ cup whole black olives, preferably Niçoise or Calamata (optional)

1. Place potatoes in large pot; cover with hot water. Cover pot; bring to a boil. Reduce heat; uncover and simmer 12 minutes, or until just tender.

2. Meanwhile, make dressing: In small jar with tight-fitting lid, shake oil, vinegar, capers, tarragon, mustard, anchovy paste, and garlic until blended.

3. Place tuna and 2 T of the dressing in a plastic reclosable bag; turn to coat. Let marinate 10 minutes.

4. With slotted spoon, remove potatoes from simmering water to medium bowl. Add beans to water; cook 3 minutes, until bright green but still crisp. Remove to bowl with potatoes; toss with 2 T of the dressing.

5. Remove tuna from bag; discard marinade. In large nonstick skillet over high heat, sear tuna 2 minutes on each side, until medium rare.

6. In large serving bowl, toss salad greens with remaining ¼ cup dressing. Arrange potatoes, beans, and olives on greens. Thinly slice tuna; arrange over salad.

S E R V E S **4**

Nutritional Information

PER SERVING: 382 cal, 31 g protein, 17 g fat, 28 g carbohydrate, 44 mg cholesterol, 122 mg sodium

SHOPPING TIP

Swiss chard is a great source of absorbable iron and beta-carotene (a cancer-fighting agent). Spinach would be a fine substitute. If possible, have your fish market shell and devein the shrimp for you. Or use frozen shrimp—it comes already shelled and deveined.

GAME PLAN

1. Bring the broth for the grits to a boil.

2. Prep the vegetables.

3. Cook the grits while stir-frying the shrimp and vegetables.

Garlicky Shrimp and Swiss Chard

1 T unsalted butter
1 red pepper, coarsely chopped
½ medium red onion, chopped
6 oz mushrooms, sliced (about 2 cups)
5 cloves garlic, minced
1 lb small shrimp, peeled and deveined
1 medium bunch Swiss chard (about 12 oz), cleaned,
    trimmed, and coarsely chopped
½ tsp salt
¼ tsp black pepper

1. Melt butter in large nonstick skillet over medium-high heat. Add red pepper, onions, mushrooms, and garlic. Cook 3 minutes, or until vegetables are tender, stirring.

2. Add remaining ingredients; cook 5 minutes, stirring.

To get the most flavor and nutrients from leafy greens, follow these tips:

Selecting   Choose crisp bunches; avoid leaves that are slimy or wilted. Stems shouldn't be limp or shriveled. To save time, it's okay to buy packaged spinach, which is already cleaned, but inspect bags for freshness.

Storing   Greens are quite perishable. They're best used within 3 to 5 days, depending on the type of leaf. Store greens, unwashed, in a plastic bag in the vegetable bin of the refrigerator.

Washing   Most greens are sandy and must be washed thoroughly. The easiest way is to trim the stems and place the leaves in a sink or large bowl full of cold water. Swirl greens around with your hands and let stand a few minutes until the grit settles to the bottom. Lift leaves out; drain the water, then repeat the process, if needed. Dry greens in a salad spinner, or lay them out on paper towels, and blot dry. There's no need to dry leaves if they are going to be cooked right away.

Trimming   Trim the thickest bottom stem from delicate greens like arugula and watercress. When cooking tougher, heartier greens (like Swiss chard, kale, and collards), the whole stem must be removed. Fold each leaf in half lengthwise, so that the stem is on the right side. Lay it on a board, then cut the stem from the leaf. •

Quick Cheese Grits

2 cans (13¾-oz size) reduced-sodium chicken broth
¾ cup quick-cooking grits
½ cup shredded sharp cheddar cheese

1. In medium nonstick skillet, over medium-high heat, bring broth to a boil.

2. Slowly stir in grits; reduce heat to low. Cover and cook 7 minutes, or until grits are creamy and thick, stirring occasionally.

3. Add cheese; stir until melted.

4. Spoon hot grits into four shallow bowls; top with shrimp mixture.

SERVES 4

Nutritional Information

PER SERVING OF SHRIMP: 152 cal, 13 g protein, 4 g fat, 9 g carbohydrate, 174 mg cholesterol, 670 mg sodium
PER SERVING OF GRITS: 133 cal, 6 g protein, 1 g fat, 24 g carbohydrate, 3 mg cholesterol, 3 mg sodium

GAME PLAN

1. Preheat oven. Cook fries and then start steak.

2. While fries cook, make the salad vinaigrette and the sauce for the steak.

Steak au Poivre

2 T olive oil
3 New York strip steaks, 1-inch thick (about 2 lb)
1½ T cracked black pepper
½ tsp salt
2 shallots, minced
¼ cup cognac or brandy
1 cup reduced-sodium beef broth
¼ cup half and half
2 T chopped fresh Italian parsley

1. Warm oil in large, heavy skillet over medium-high heat until hot but not smoking.

2. Sprinkle steaks with salt and pepper; cook in skillet for 6 minutes on each side. Remove to a plate.

3. Drain and discard excess oil from skillet. In same skillet over medium heat, cook shallots—stirring for 30 seconds, until softened.

4. Add cognac to skillet. Still over medium heat; simmer 30 seconds, until almost evaporated.

5. Increase heat to high; add broth and cook 5 minutes, stirring a few times until sauce is reduced by about ½.

6. Add half and half; bring to a boil. Reduce heat; simmer 3 minutes. Remove from heat; stir in parsley.

7. Slice steaks, arrange on serving plate. Spoon warm sauce over slices.

Green Salad with Tarragon Vinaigrette

1 bag (10 oz) salad greens
¼ cup extra-virgin olive oil
1 clove garlic, minced
2 T fresh lemon juice
3 T chopped fresh tarragon
1 T Dijon mustard

In large serving bowl, whisk dressing ingredients until well blended. Add greens; toss well.

SERVES 4

Nutritional Information

PER SERVING OF STEAK: 246 cal, 18 g protein, 14 g fat, 2 g carbohydrate, 51 mg cholesterol, 332 mg sodium
PER SERVING OF SALAD: 138 cal, 1 g protein, 14 g fat, 4 g carbohydrate, 0 mg cholesterol, 56 mg sodium

COOKING TIP

To crack peppercorns, put them in a plastic bag on the kitchen counter and hit gently with the bottom of a heavy pot. You can also use regular black pepper, or omit the pepper entirely for the kids.

GAME PLAN

1. Preheat the oven and make the muffin batter.

2. Prep the salad ingredients.

Warm Chicken and Arugula Salad

2 T olive oil
*1¼ lb boneless, skinless chicken tenders,
    cut into 1-inch chunks*
1 clove garlic, minced
3 T orange juice
2 T balsamic vinegar
1 T Dijon mustard

¼ tsp salt
*2 medium bunches arugula (about 8
    oz), cleaned and trimmed*
2 oranges, peeled and sectioned
½ small bulb fennel, diced (optional)
1 log (4 oz) goat cheese, crumbled

1. Warm 1 T of the oil in large nonstick skillet over medium-high heat. Cook chicken chunks 4 minutes, stirring. Add garlic; cook 2 minutes more, stirring.

2. Reduce heat to low; stir in orange juice, vinegar, mustard, and salt. Slowly stir in remaining 1 T oil until combined.

3. Divide arugula among 4 plates. Sprinkle with orange sections and fennel. Spoon warm chicken mixture over salad; top with crumbled goat cheese.

Mini Double Corn Muffins

1 pkg (8 oz) corn-muffin mix
1 egg white
⅓ cup skim milk
½ cup frozen corn kernels (no need to thaw)

1. Preheat oven to 425°F. In medium bowl, combine mix with egg white, skim milk, and corn. Divide batter among 12 mini-muffin cups; let sit 5 minutes.

2. Bake 12 minutes, or until puffed and golden.

SERVES **4**

Nutritional Information

PER SERVING OF SALAD: 429 cal, 47 g protein, 21 g fat, 13 g carbohydrate, 126 mg cholesterol, 380 mg sodium
PER SERVING OF 3 MINI MUFFINS: 267 cal, 5 g protein, 6 g fat, 47 g carbohydrate, trace cholesterol, 503 mg sodium

Seared Salmon with Caramelized Carrots and Onions
with Sesame Egg Noodles

 GAME PLAN

1. Preheat the oven and boil water for noodles.

2. Chop the carrots and onions.

3. While the noodles cook, quickly sear the salmon fillets and sauté the vegetables.

Seared Salmon with Caramelized Carrots and Onions

4 center-cut salmon fillets, 1-inch thick (about 1½ lb), skinned and boned
¼ tsp salt
¼ tsp black pepper
2 T olive oil
1 T butter
2 large carrots, thinly sliced
2 medium onions, thinly sliced
1 tsp granulated sugar
1 T reduced-sodium soy sauce
1 T cider vinegar

1. Preheat oven to 200°F. Sprinkle salmon with salt and pepper.

2. In large heavy skillet, warm 1 T of the oil over medium-high heat, until hot but not smoking. Add salmon, skinned-side down; cook 3 minutes per side, until browned and just cooked through. With spatula, carefully remove to ovenproof plate. Cover with foil; place in preheated oven to keep warm.

3. Pour off fat; wipe out skillet with paper towel. Warm butter and remaining 1 T oil over medium-high heat, until butter melts. Add carrots, onion, and sugar. Increase heat to high; cook about 8 minutes, until vegetables are tender, stirring often. Reduce heat if vegetables start to burn. Stir in soy sauce and vinegar. Serve salmon topped with vegetables.

Sesame Egg Noodles

12 oz wide egg noodles
2 T chopped scallions
1½ T Asian sesame oil
¼ tsp salt

1. Cook noodles according to package directions.

2. Drain; return to cooking pot and toss with 2 T chopped scallions, 1½ T Asian sesame oil, and ¼ tsp salt.

SERVES 4

Nutritional Information

PER SERVING OF SALMON: 379 cal, 35 g protein, 21 g fat, 12 g carbohydrate, 101 mg cholesterol, 409 mg sodium
PER SERVING OF NOODLES: 312 cal, 10 g protein, 8 g fat, 50 g carbohydrate, 66 mg cholesterol, 148 mg sodium

GAME PLAN

1. Preheat the oven and make the dressing.

2. Warm the tortillas, while sautéing the filling.

Lamb-and-Pepper Wraps

BALSAMIC DRESSING
¼ cup extra-virgin olive oil
2 T balsamic vinegar
2 tsp Dijon mustard
¼ tsp salt
¼ tsp black pepper

WRAP AND FILLING
8 large (10-inch size) flour tortillas
1 T olive oil
1 lb lean lamb (loin), cut into thin strips
¼ tsp salt
¼ tsp black pepper
1 red and 1 yellow pepper, seeded and thinly sliced
1 small onion, thinly sliced
3 cloves garlic, minced

1. Preheat oven to 400°F. In medium glass measuring cup, combine all dressing ingredients; set aside.

2. Stack tortillas flat and wrap in foil; warm in oven about 10 minutes.

3. Meanwhile, warm oil in large nonstick skillet over high heat. Slice lamb into strips and sprinkle with salt and black pepper; stir-fry in skillet for 2 minutes.

4. Add red and yellow peppers, onions, and garlic; stir-fry 3 minutes, until vegetables are softened and lamb is cooked through.

5. Remove from heat; stir in ½ cup of the balsamic dressing. Reserve remaining dressing for salad.

6. Spoon lamb mixture on warmed tortillas. Add Balsamic Greens (see recipe below) and roll up.

SHOPPING TIP

Dark salad greens, like romaine and loose-leaf, provide the most vitamin A and folic acid.

Balsamic Greens

1 bag (10 oz) precleaned salad greens
Reserved salad dressing
2 oz feta cheese, crumbled

1. In medium serving bowl, toss salad greens with reserved balsamic dressing.

2. Sprinkle with feta cheese.

3. To make wraps, spread lamb mixture on tortilla, top with greens and feta and roll up.

SERVES **4**

Nutritional Information

PER SERVING OF WRAP: 481 cal, 29 g protein, 16 g fat, 54 g carbohydrate, 65 mg cholesterol, 600 mg sodium

Dijon Pork Chops
with Buttermilk Mashed Potatoes

 GAME PLAN

1. Put water on to boil for potatoes.

2. Mince the shallot and cook the chops.

3. Start making the sauce while potatoes boil; mash the potatoes while the sauce reduces.

Dijon Pork Chops

4 boneless pork chops, ¾-inch thick (about 1⅓ lb)
½ tsp salt
¼ tsp black pepper
1 T olive oil
2 T butter, diced
1 large shallot, minced
½ cup reduced-sodium chicken broth
½ cup dry white wine
1 T Dijon mustard

1. Season pork with ¼ tsp of the salt and ⅛ tsp of the pepper. Warm oil in large heavy skillet over medium-high heat, until hot but not smoking. Cook pork about 5 minutes per side, until browned and cooked through. Remove to plate; cover to keep warm.

2. Melt 1 tsp of the butter in same skillet over medium heat. Cook shallot 1 minute; add broth and wine, stirring to scrape up any browned bits. Increase heat to high; boil about 5 minutes, until reduced by half. Whisk in mustard.

3. Remove skillet from heat; whisk in remaining butter, a few pieces at a time. Stir in any juices from meat plate. Add remaining ¼ tsp salt and the ⅛ tsp pepper. Serve pork drizzled with sauce from pan.

Buttermilk Mashed Potatoes

1½ lb small red potatoes, unpeeled and quartered
½ cup buttermilk
1 T butter
½ tsp salt
⅛ tsp black pepper

1. Bring medium pot of hot salted water to a boil. Cook potatoes about 15 minutes, until tender. In liquid measuring cup, combine buttermilk, butter, salt, and black pepper.

2. Drain potatoes; return to pot and mash in buttermilk mixture to a chunky consistency.

SERVES **4**

Nutritional Information

PER SERVING OF PORK CHOP: 477 cal, 28 g protein, 37 g fat, 2 g carbohydrate, 117 mg cholesterol, 487 mg sodium
PER SERVING OF MASHED POTATOES: 235 cal, 5 g protein, 3 g fat, 47 g carbohydrate, 9 mg cholesterol, 308 mg sodium

Pasta with Greens and White Beans
with Pesto Toasts

**SHOPPING AND
COOKING TIP**

*Arugula is delicate,
so add it at the end
of the cooking time—
just to wilt. Substi-
tute watercress or
spinach, if desired.*

GAME PLAN

1. Preheat the broiler, then prep the vegetables.

2. Make the sauce while pasta water comes to a boil.

3. Broil the toasts while pasta cooks.

Pasta with Greens and White Beans

¾ lb medium shell or bow-tie pasta
1 T olive oil
6 plum tomatoes, diced
3 cloves garlic, minced
¼ tsp red pepper flakes
1 can (19 oz) cannellini beans, drained and rinsed
1 cup reduced-sodium chicken broth
1 tsp salt
1 large bunch arugula (about 6 oz), cleaned, trimmed,
    and coarsely chopped
¼ cup grated Parmesan cheese

1. Cook pasta according to package directions; drain.

2. Warm oil in large nonstick skillet over medium-high heat. Add tomatoes, garlic, and pepper flakes; cook 3 minutes, stirring. Add beans, broth, and salt; simmer 5 minutes. Stir in arugula; remove from heat.

3. In large serving bowl, toss drained pasta with sauce. Sprinkle with cheese.

Bravo Beans

Canned beans are a smart choice for family meals. Beans are a low-fat, concentrated source of many vitamins and minerals. Just one cup provides nearly ½ of the daily requirement of fiber, ⅓ of the daily requirement of protein, and 92 percent of the daily requirement of folic acid. Folic acid, or folate, may help reduce the risk of certain birth defects by up to 50 percent. Research has also found that folate may help protect against heart disease and stroke. •

Pesto Toasts

1 small loaf Italian bread
Prepared pesto

Preheat broiler. Cut bread into 8 diagonal slices. Lightly spread each slice with prepared pesto. Broil until toasted.

SERVES 4

Nutritional Information

PER SERVING OF PASTA: 292 cal, 13 g protein, 7 g fat, 45 g carbohydrate, 5 mg cholesterol, 788 mg sodium
PER 2 SLICES OF TOAST: 218 cal, 7 g protein, 6 g fat, 33 g carbohydrate, 4 mg cholesterol, 485 mg sodium

Freeze-Ahead Meals

● ● ●

How Freeze-Ahead Meals Work

Cook when you have the time. Don't cook when you're rushed. That's the secret to freeze-ahead success.

In this section we show you how to prepare meals in quantity when you have a few spare hours—such as on weekends or one evening a week—and then freeze the meals in suitable portions. You may not be wild about the idea of chunks of time needed to make up these extra-useful recipes—but come 6 o'clock on a harried work night, you'll be able to play with the kids or relax on the sofa instead of standing in front of the stove.

This section offers two kinds of freeze-ahead meals. Both make family dining surprisingly simple.

Big Batch

Big-batch recipes make from 8 to 12 servings. These are mostly soups and stews that cook virtually unattended. Freeze them in various-size containers, some for full family meals, others as single servings. (Of course, if you like, you can serve these meal recipes the night you cook them. Or, you could refrigerate—not freeze—until tomorrow and then reheat.)

Master Plans

For these recipes, you make one master recipe (for example, roast two whole chickens), and then from that you are able to make six completely different meals, yielding as many as 36 servings.

Tips for Freezing, Defrosting, and Reheating

You can freeze any of the recipes in this section for up to three months. Frozen foods fare best when wrapped and stored properly. Here are some tips:

- *Cool foods first:* The food should be at room temperature so it freezes quickly and won't raise the temperature of your freezer.

- *Label each package:* Include name of dish, the date prepared, and defrosting and cooking instructions, just in case you misplace the recipe. You can write directly on aluminum foil with a permanent-marker pen.

- *Thaw safely:* Thaw frozen foods still wrapped in foil in the refrigerator on a tray. Some dishes—minus the foil—can be defrosted in the microwave. Thawing food at room temperature encourages spoilage and the growth of bacteria. When defrosting, allow at least two days for the food to thaw in the refrigerator (thawing at room temperature can cause health problems) or defrost and reheat in the microwave.

- *Reheat all the way through:* Times vary depending on the size of container and power of your microwave. If mixture seems too thick when reheating, add a little water.

Big-Batch Dinners

• • •

Quick to prepare and absolutely delicious, this is a soup you'll make again and again. We've made this soup mild to please younger palates; to increase the heat, add another jalapeño and use spicy salsa.

8 small corn tortillas
4 boneless, skinless, whole chicken
 breasts, cut into 1½ inch chunks
1 tsp salt
½ tsp black pepper
3 T vegetable oil
1 large onion, chopped
2 cloves garlic, minced
2 jalapeño peppers, seeded and minced
2 tsp ground cumin
¼ tsp cayenne pepper

4 cans (13¾-oz size) reduced-sodium
 chicken broth
1 jar (7 oz) mild prepared salsa
4 fresh plum tomatoes, cut into large
 dice
1 cup frozen corn kernels
¼ cup shredded Monterey Jack cheese
¼ cup prepared guacamole, optional
 garnish
½ cup chopped fresh cilantro, optional
 garnish

1. Preheat oven to 400°F. Cut tortillas into wide strips; place on ungreased baking sheet. Bake 10 minutes, until lightly browned and crisp, shaking pan gently twice during cooking to prevent sticking.

2. Sprinkle chicken with salt and black pepper. Meanwhile, warm 2 T of the oil in large Dutch oven over medium heat. Add chicken chunks in 2 batches, about 6 minutes per batch, until browned on all sides but not cooked through. Add remaining T oil as needed. Remove to plate.

3. Reduce heat to medium-low. Cook onion 5 minutes, until softened, stirring. Add garlic, jalapeño, cumin, and cayenne; cook 1 minute, stirring. Add broth and salsa. Increase heat to high; bring to a boil. Reduce heat and simmer 10 minutes, uncovered, to blend flavors.

4. Add chicken and any plate juices to pot. Cover pot to bring back to a simmer; continue simmering, partially covered, about 7 minutes, until chicken is cooked through.

DINNER PLAN

1. Remove half of soup to microwave-proof container. Cool, then freeze.

2. Bring remaining soup back to a simmer; add tomatoes and corn. Simmer 2 minutes, to warm through.

3. To serve, ladle soup into bowls and top with baked tortilla strips and cheese; garnish with guacamole and cilantro, if desired.

Reheating Instructions   Defrost in refrigerator. Reheat in microwave or on stovetop. Add corn and tomatoes when reheating. Garnish servings with tortilla strips, cheese, guacamole, and cilantro, if desired.

MAKES **2** MEALS FOR A FAMILY OF **4**

Nutritional Information

PER SERVING: 247 cal, 19 g protein, 9 g fat, 24 g carbohydrate, 40 mg cholesterol, 508 mg sodium

Here's a soup especially for the kids—it's brimming with the things they love. Older children can help form the meatballs. Keep in mind that the more gently you handle the mixture, the more tender the finished product will be.

4 slices whole-wheat bread, crusts
   removed
½ cup low-fat milk
1 lb lean ground beef
2 large eggs
1 tsp salt
¼ tsp black pepper
1 T vegetable oil
1 medium onion, finely chopped

1 cup baby carrots
⅓ cup dry sherry
2 cans (13¾-oz size) reduced-
   sodium beef broth
2 bay leaves
1 tsp Worcestershire sauce
1 cup (4 oz) alphabet pasta or
   other small shape
1 cup frozen green peas

1. In medium bowl, soak bread in milk. Gently squeeze bread, pour off milk. In small bowl, lightly beat eggs, salt, and pepper. Add egg mixture to bread, then add beef. Mix with hands until blended. Form meatballs about ¾ inch in diameter. (You should have about 40.)

2. Warm oil in large Dutch oven over medium-low heat. Cook onion and carrots about 5 minutes, until softened, stirring. Add sherry; cook 3 minutes, until liquid is almost gone. Add broth, bay leaves, Worcestershire, and 4 cups water. Increase heat to high; bring to a boil. Reduce heat and simmer 5 minutes, uncovered, to blend flavors.

3. Carefully drop meatballs into simmering broth; cook 8 minutes. Add water to cover meatballs, if needed.

DINNER PLAN

1. Remove ½ of soup (about 6 cups) to microwave-proof container. Cool, then freeze.

2. Bring remaining soup back to a simmer; add pasta and peas. Simmer until pasta is done.

Reheating Instructions   Defrost in refrigerator. Reheat in microwave or on stovetop. Cook 1 cup pasta separately; add with peas when reheating.

MAKES **2** MEALS FOR A FAMILY OF **4**

Nutritional Information

PER SERVING OF 5 MEATBALLS: 292 cal, 18 g protein, 12 g fat, 21 g carbohydrate, 92 mg cholesterol, 431 mg sodium

Indian-Summer Corn Chowder

COOKING TIP

Combining the cornstarch with the evaporated milk before adding it to the soup helps keep the cornstarch from lumping.

Pureed winter squash (available in your grocer's freezer) adds a vibrant golden color and lush texture to this super-healthy salute to autumn.

2 tsp olive oil
2 red onions, diced
3 cloves garlic, minced
2 red peppers, diced
1 T fresh thyme or 1 tsp dried
1 large russet potato, peeled and cut into small dice
3 zucchini, quartered lengthwise and cut into ½-inch-thick slices
2 tsp salt

1 tsp black pepper
2 cans (13¾-oz size) reduced-sodium chicken broth
1 pkg (10 oz) frozen winter squash, thawed
3 pkg (10-oz size) frozen corn kernels
1 can (12 oz) nonfat evaporated milk
2 T cornstarch
2 T chopped fresh chives, optional garnish

1. **Warm oil** in large Dutch oven over medium-low heat. Cook onion 5 minutes, until softened, stirring. Add garlic, red pepper, and thyme; cook 3 minutes, stirring.

2. **Add potato,** zucchini, salt, and black pepper, stirring to coat. Add broth. Increase heat to high; bring to a boil. Reduce heat and simmer about 10 minutes, covered, until vegetables are tender.

3. **Stir** in squash and simmer, uncovered, about 5 minutes. Meanwhile, in small bowl, combine milk and cornstarch.

4. **Increase heat** to high; bring to a boil. Add milk mixture and corn, cook about 1 minute, stirring constantly, until soup is thickened.

DINNER PLAN

Remove ½ of soup to microwave-proof container. Cool, then freeze. Serve remaining soup. Sprinkle servings with chives, if desired.

Reheating Instructions   Defrost in refrigerator. Reheat in microwave or on stovetop. Garnish servings with additional chives, if desired.

MAKES **2** MEALS FOR A FAMILY OF **4**

Nutritional Information

PER SERVING: 199 cal, 9 g protein, 2 g fat, 41 g carbohydrate, 2 mg cholesterol, 617 mg sodium

Hearty Beef Vegetable Stew

This satisfying stew is ideal for make ahead; it just gets better when reheated. Browning the meat first gives a richer flavor, so don't skip this step. Make sure the beef is only lightly coated with flour, otherwise the flour will burn in the pan. Serve with egg noodles and a green salad.

½ cup all-purpose flour
1 tsp salt
½ tsp black pepper
4 lb boneless beef chuck, cut into 1½-inch cubes
4 T olive oil
3 large carrots, cut into ½-inch chunks
2 parsnips or turnips, cut into ½-inch chunks
3 leeks, thickly sliced

2 cloves garlic, chopped
1 can (14 oz) plum tomatoes, with juice
2 cans (13¾-oz size) reduced-sodium beef broth
2 tsp fresh thyme or 1 tsp dried
2 dried bay leaves
1 small butternut squash, peeled and cut into 1-inch chunks

1. On plate or wax paper, combine flour, ½ tsp of the salt and all of the pepper. Lightly coat beef cubes, shaking off excess.

2. Warm 3 T of the oil in large Dutch oven over medium-high heat. Cook beef in 3 batches, about 3 minutes per batch, until browned on all sides. Remove to large plate. With a paper towel, wipe the bottom of the pot to remove any flour lumps.

3. Reduce heat to medium-low. Warm remaining 1 T oil; cook carrots, parsnips, leeks, and garlic about 10 minutes, until softened, stirring.

4. Return beef to pot, along with any plate juices. Add tomatoes, broth, thyme, bay leaves, and 2 cups water, stirring to scrape up brown bits. Increase heat to high; bring to a boil. Reduce heat and simmer, uncovered, about 1 hour, until beef is almost tender, stirring occasionally. Add additional water to cover, if needed.

5. Add squash and remaining ½ tsp salt; bring back to a simmer. Cook, partially covered, about 18 minutes, until squash is fork-tender.

DINNER PLAN

Remove ½ of stew to microwave-proof container. Cool, then freeze. Serve remaining stew.

Reheating Instructions

Defrost in refrigerator. Reheat in microwave or on stovetop.

MAKES 2 MEALS FOR A FAMILY OF 4 TO 6

Nutritional Information

PER SERVING: 395 cal, 44 g protein, 17 g fat, 16 g carbohydrate, 121 mg cholesterol, 399 mg sodium

Tuscan White Beans with Parmesan Crostini

White beans become creamy as they cook, resulting in a rich, velvety soup. Keep taste-testing the beans as they simmer—cooking time varies with the age of the legumes. If you prefer a thinner consistency, stir in additional water as the soup cooks.

1½ lb dried Great Northern or small
 white beans
2 tsp olive oil
2 oz pancetta or bacon, chopped
4 medium carrots, thinly sliced
4 cloves garlic, chopped
3 medium stalks celery, thinly sliced
2 medium onions, chopped
3 fresh sage leaves, chopped, or 1 tsp
 dried

1 large can (48 oz) or 5½ cups
 reduced-sodium chicken broth
½ medium savoy cabbage, cored and
 chopped into small pieces
2 tsp salt
½ tsp black pepper
8 thick slices Italian bread (about 6
 oz)
¼ cup grated Parmesan cheese

1. In large bowl, cover beans with cold water; soak overnight in refrigerator. Add additional water to cover, if needed. Drain; set beans aside.

2. Warm oil in large Dutch oven over medium-low heat. Cook pancetta 5 minutes, until browned, stirring. Add carrots, garlic, celery, onion, and sage; cook about 10 minutes, until vegetables are softened, stirring. Add beans, broth, cabbage, salt, pepper, and 4 cups water. Add additional water to cover, if needed.

3. Increase heat to high; bring to a boil. Reduce heat and simmer, partially covered, for about 1½ hours, until beans are very tender.

DINNER PLAN

1. Remove ½ of soup to microwave-proof container. Cool, then freeze. Serve remaining soup.

2. For crostini: Preheat broiler. Broil bread slices until browned on both sides. Place 2 pieces toast atop soup in each serving bowl; sprinkle with grated cheese. Heat from soup will melt cheese.

Reheating Instructions

Defrost in refrigerator. Reheat in microwave or on stovetop. Broil additional cheese toasts.

MAKES **2** MEALS FOR A FAMILY OF **4** TO **6**

Nutritional Information

PER SERVING: 241 cal, 13 g protein, 6 g fat, 34 g carbohydrate, 7 mg cholesterol, 737 mg sodium

Country Captain Chicken Curry

This flavorful stew is an American variation on a traditional Indian dish. To make enough for two meals, buy a whole, cut-up chicken and four extra pieces. (We like to use drumsticks to please the kids.) Serve over rice with a green salad.

5 lb bone-in chicken pieces (about 1 whole chicken, cut up, plus 4 additional pieces)
⅓ cup all-purpose flour
1 tsp salt
¼ tsp black pepper
¼ tsp paprika
4 T olive oil
2 large onions, chopped

2 green peppers, chopped
2 T curry powder
1 can (28 oz) crushed plum tomatoes
1 can (13¾-oz) reduced-sodium chicken broth
2 T chopped fresh Italian parsley
½ cup blanched almonds, optional garnish
½ cup golden raisins, optional garnish

1. Rinse and pat dry chicken. On plate or wax paper, combine flour, salt, black pepper, and paprika. Lightly coat chicken pieces, shaking off excess.

2. Warm 2 T of the oil in very large Dutch oven over medium heat. Cook chicken in 2 batches, about 10 minutes per batch, until browned on all sides. Add additional 1 T oil as needed. Remove to large plate. With paper towel, wipe bottom of pot to remove any flour lumps.

3. Reduce heat to low. Warm remaining 1 T oil; cook onion, green pepper, and curry about 10 minutes, until softened, stirring.

4. Return chicken to the pot; add tomatoes, broth, and 1 cup water. Increase heat to high; bring to a boil. Reduce heat and simmer, partially covered, about 25 minutes, until chicken is cooked through.

DINNER PLAN

1. Remove ½ of stew to microwave-proof container. Cool, then freeze.

2. Skim excess fat off surface of remaining stew. Top servings with parsley; garnish with almonds and raisins, if desired.

Reheating Instructions

Skim any fat off surface of stew. Defrost in refrigerator. Reheat in microwave or on stovetop. Garnish servings with additional parsley, almonds, and raisins, if desired.

MAKES **2** MEALS FOR A FAMILY OF **4** TO **6**

Nutritional Information

PER SERVING: 289 cal, 24 g protein, 16 g fat, 12 g carbohydrate, 69 mg cholesterol, 418 mg sodium

Luscious Lentil Soup with Zesty Lime Cream

This hearty soup, full of nutritious, fast-cooking lentils, is ample enough for three nights' worth of family suppers. Cut your prep time by using a food processor to chop the vegetables. (For a spicier version, leave the seeds in the jalapeño.)

3 T olive oil
3 medium onions, chopped
3 medium red peppers, chopped
3 cloves garlic, minced
2 jalapeño peppers, seeded and finely chopped
1 T minced fresh oregano, or 1 tsp dried
1 T ground cumin
1½ tsp ground coriander
4 cups red or brown lentils, rinsed and picked over

2 large cans (2 pints, 14 oz each) reduced-sodium chicken broth
1 can (28–35¼ oz) tomatoes
1¼ tsp salt
½ cup coarsely chopped fresh cilantro

ZESTY LIME CREAM
⅓ cup light sour cream
1 T lime juice

1. Warm oil in 10-quart pot or Dutch oven over medium heat. Add onion and cook for 3 minutes. Add red pepper, garlic, jalapeño, oregano, cumin, and coriander; cook for 10 minutes, until vegetables are soft, stirring frequently.

2. Add lentils, broth, tomatoes with liquid (breaking them up with a spoon), and 2 cups water. Increase heat and bring to a boil. Reduce heat and simmer for 30 minutes, or until lentils are tender, stirring occasionally (red lentils may take less time than brown). Stir in salt.

3. Remove ⅓ of the soup to food processor fitted with metal blade. Puree soup by pulsing on-and-off. Stir puree back into soup in pot, along with cilantro.

4. For lime cream: In small bowl, mix sour cream and lime juice; set aside.

DINNER PLAN

1. Put ⅔ of soup (about 14 cups) into 2 separate microwave-proof containers; cool, then freeze for later use.

2. Rewarm remaining soup before serving, if needed. Top each serving with a spoonful of lime cream.

Reheating Instructions

Defrost in refrigerator. Reheat in microwave or on stovetop. Make additional lime cream.

MAKES 3 MEALS FOR FAMILY OF 4

Nutritional Information

PER SERVING: 178 cal, 9 g protein, 6 g fat, 23 g carbohydrate, 5 mg cholesterol, 901 mg sodium

Autumn Chicken
and Dill Cornmeal Dumplings

COOKING TIP

To wash leeks, trim ends and slice them lengthwise first, then rinse in a strainer with cold water.

For this old-fashioned favorite, we kept all the fabulous flavor but lost some of the fat by removing the chicken skin.

CHICKEN
5 lb chicken legs and thighs, skinned and patted dry
½ cup all-purpose flour
4 T olive oil
4 large leeks, cut into 1-inch slices and cleaned
6 medium carrots, sliced

4 stalks celery, sliced
2 tart red apples, unpeeled, cut into thick wedges
3 cups chicken broth
1 cup apple juice
2 T finely chopped fresh dill
½ tsp salt
Pinch black pepper

1. In large plastic or paper bag, coat chicken with flour in 2 batches, shaking off excess. Place in single layer on wax paper.

2. Warm 3 tablespoons of the oil in 8-quart Dutch oven over medium heat. Add chicken in batches so that pan is not too crowded. Cook for 15 to 20 minutes per batch, or until browned on all sides. Remove to large plate.

3. Warm remaining 1 tablespoon of oil in same pan over medium heat. Add leeks and cook for 5 minutes, or until lightly browned, stirring to scrape up brown bits. Add carrots, celery, and apple wedges; cook for 4 minutes, or until slightly softened. Add browned chicken, broth, juice, and dill. Cover; increase heat and bring to a boil. Reduce heat and simmer for 15 minutes.

4. While chicken cooks, make dumpling batter (recipe follows).

Dill Cornmeal Dumplings

Homey dumplings, accented with a touch of dill, are a perfect topping for the savory chicken and leek stew. This recipe makes enough for half of the stew; prepare another batch when you reheat the other half of the stew on another night.

1¼ cups all-purpose flour
⅓ cup yellow cornmeal
1 T finely chopped fresh dill
2½ tsp baking powder
½ tsp salt
3 T chilled vegetable shortening
1 cup lowfat milk

1. In medium bowl, combine first 5 ingredients.

2. With 2 knives or your fingers, cut in shortening until mixture resembles coarse cornmeal. Add milk; stir with a fork, just until mixture holds together.

3. With a large spoon, drop dumpling batter in 8 spoonfuls over half of prepared, hot stew. (See dinner plan below.) Simmer dumplings in stew over medium-low heat, covered, for about 16 minutes. Dumplings are done when a skewer inserted in the center comes out cleanly.

DINNER PLAN

Before adding dumplings, remove ½ of stew to microwave-proof container; cool, then freeze for later use.

Reheating Instructions

Defrost in refrigerator. When defrosted, place in deep, 10-inch skillet. Make another batch of dumplings, and cook as directed above.

MAKES **2** MEALS FOR FAMILY OF **4** OR **5**

Nutritional information

PER SERVING: 629 cal, 47 g protein, 28 g fat, 46 g carbohydrate, 150 mg cholesterol, 893 mg sodium

Master Recipes

• • •

Master Recipe for Cider-Braised Pork Loin

For Use in: North Carolina Pulled Pork Sandwiches
• Chorizo Chili • New England Pork and Beans

SHOPPING TIP

Have your butcher roll and tie the roast for you and ask him for 1½ pounds of pork bones, which will be used to flavor the chili and the baked beans. (The bones needn't come from the roast.)

COOKING TIP

Kosher salt is ideal for coating roasts, but you may use table salt, if you like.

8 cloves garlic, chopped
2 T kosher salt
2 T Dijon mustard
4 lb boneless pork loin, rolled and tied
2 cups apple cider

1. In small bowl, combine garlic, salt, and mustard; mash with a fork into a paste. With your hands, spread all over the pork. Cover with plastic; refrigerate overnight.

2. Preheat oven to 400°F. In large roasting pan, roast pork, fat side up, 40 minutes. Reduce heat to 350°F. Pour cider over pork; cook 35 minutes, until internal temperature is 155°F, basting occasionally. Remove from oven; let stand 15 minutes.

3. Strain roasting-pan juices into a small plastic container (you should have about 1¼ cups). Add to container juices that accumulate as pork rests. Wrap roast in aluminum foil; refrigerate overnight. Cover and refrigerate roasting liquid. Refrigerate pork bones.

4. The next day:

• Slice off ⅓ of the roast (about 1 lb) and cut into ½-inch cubes; reserve for Chorizo Chili.

• Cut off 1¼ lb (just over half of remaining piece) and finely shred; reserve for Pulled Pork Sandwiches.

• Slice remaining pork (about ¾ lb) into thin strips; reserve for Pork and Beans.

North Carolina Pulled Pork Sandwiches

1 can (8 oz) tomato sauce
¾ cup cider vinegar
½ cup brown sugar
1 clove garlic, chopped
2 T Worcestershire sauce
1 T dry mustard

1 tsp powdered ginger
Pinch red-pepper flakes (optional)
1¼ lb Cider-Braised Pork Loin,
    finely shredded (See Master Recipe)
4 to 6 hamburger buns or hard rolls

SHOPPING TIP

To save time, you may substitute 1½ cups of your favorite bottled BBQ sauce for the first eight ingredients. The rolls can be bought ahead and frozen; warm them before serving.

1. In medium saucepan over high heat, combine first 8 ingredients. Bring to a boil; reduce heat to low and simmer 30 minutes, until thick and slightly darkened. (No need to simmer if using canned sauce.)

2. Stir in shredded pork. Cool completely.

FREEZING PLAN

- Freeze in any size plastic container for single-serve or family dinners.

DINING PLAN

1. Whenever you're planning to enjoy, defrost for 2 days in refrigerator, or on the spot in the microwave.

2. Reheat in microwave, or transfer to saucepan and simmer gently over low heat until heated through.

3. Split rolls; warm or toast in oven. Put a generous portion of pork between buns.

SERVES 4 TO 6

Nutritional Information

PER SERVING: 403 cal, 25 g protein, 11 g fat, 51 g carbohydrate, 61 mg cholesterol, 1170 mg sodium

Spicy Chorizo Chili

SHOPPING TIP

Chorizo is a mildly spiced Spanish sausage—if it's unavailable, use another dry-cured, firm link variety.

For a hearty fall meal, serve this flavor-packed chili over white rice and top with a dollop of sour cream and chopped fresh cilantro.

¾ lb pork bones
2 small links chorizo (about ⅓ lb), thinly sliced
1 medium onion, diced
1 medium red or green bell pepper, diced
1 small jalapeño pepper, seeded and minced (optional)
1¼ cups reserved-pork roasting juices
1 can (13¾ oz) reduced-sodium beef broth

1 T chili powder
2 tsp ground cumin
1 tsp salt
3 cans (15-oz size) red kidney beans, drained and rinsed
1 lb Cider-Braised Pork Loin (See Master Recipe), cut into ½ inch cubes

1. **Warm 8-quart** Dutch oven over high heat. Sear pork bones about 10 minutes, turning until brown on all sides; set aside.

2. **In same pot** over medium heat, cook chorizo, onion, bell and jalapeño peppers about 5 minutes, until vegetables are softened, stirring occasionally. Return bones to pot; add roasting juices, broth, chili powder, cumin, and salt. Bring to boil over high heat, reduce heat and simmer 20 minutes.

3. **Add beans** and diced pork; simmer 15 minutes longer. Let cool completely; remove and discard bones before freezing.

FREEZING PLAN

• Freeze in any size plastic container for single-serve or family dinners.

DINNER PLAN

1. Defrost for 2 days in refrigerator, or on the spot in microwave.

2. Reheat in microwave, or transfer to saucepan and simmer gently over low heat until heated through. Meanwhile, cook rice, if desired.

SERVES 6

Nutritional Information

PER SERVING: 311 cal, 17 g protein, 8 g fat, 44 g carbohydrate, 17 mg cholesterol, 1000 mg sodium

New England Pork and Beans

An old-fashioned dish you can put in the oven and forget for 3 hours—great for weekend cooking.

COOKING TIP

Stir in the salt once dish is cooked; adding it during cooking prevents the beans from softening.

1 lb dried baby lima beans or navy beans
4 strips bacon, thinly sliced crosswise
1 medium onion, diced
2 cups apple cider
½ cup molasses
2 dried bay leaves

1 tsp chopped fresh thyme or 2 tsp dried thyme
¼ tsp ground cloves
¾ lb pork bones
¾ lb Cider-Braised Pork Loin (See Master Recipe), cut into thin strips
1½ tsp salt

1. Rinse and pick over beans. Cover with cold water; soak overnight. Drain.

2. Preheat oven to 300°F. In 8-quart Dutch oven, sauté bacon slices until crisp. Add onion; cook 3 minutes, stirring. Add beans, cider, molasses, bay leaves, thyme, cloves, and 2 cups water. Lay bones on top of beans; press down lightly. Place in oven; cook 3½ hours, covered. Do not stir.

3. Remove bones; let them cool slightly. Remove meat from bones; gently stir meat into pot along with reserved pork strips. Add salt and an additional 1 cup water, or to desired consistency. Return to oven; bake 30 minutes, uncovered. Cool completely before freezing.

FREEZING PLAN

• Freeze in any size plastic container for single-serve or family dinners.

DINNER PLAN

1. Defrost for 2 days in refrigerator, or in microwave.

2. Reheat in microwave, or transfer to saucepan, cover, and simmer gently over low heat until heated through.

SERVES 6

Nutritional Information

PER SERVING: 515 cal, 33 g protein, 10 g fat, 73 g carbohydrate, 56 mg cholesterol, 1100 mg sodium

Master Recipe for 3-Cheese Sauce

For Use in: Risotto with Sun-Dried Tomatoes • Cheesy Chicken Casserole • Baked Penne with Autumn Vegetables

COOKING TIP

After stirring in the cheeses, heat the sauce gently—boiling will cause it to curdle.

2 cups (about 8 oz) grated fontina cheese
2 cups (about 8 oz) grated Gruyère cheese
1 cup (about 4 oz) grated Parmesan cheese
4 large eggs
2 cans (12-oz size) evaporated skim milk
½ tsp hot-pepper sauce
1 tsp salt
2 tsp dry mustard
4 T (half a stick) unsalted butter, cut into 4 pieces

1. In medium bowl, combine all cheeses; set aside.

2. In medium saucepan, whisk eggs, 1½ cans of the milk, pepper sauce, and salt until well blended. In cup, mix dry mustard with 2 tsp water until smooth; add to pot. Over low heat, cook about 5 minutes, until hot but not simmering, whisking often.

3. Still over low heat, add ½ of the cheese mixture to saucepan; whisk until smooth. Gradually add butter pieces, remaining cheese, and ½ can milk; continue cooking about 5 minutes, until combined and slightly thickened, whisking often. Do not simmer.

4. Remove from heat; cover and let stand at room temperature. (If desired, refrigerate, tightly covered, to use next day.) Use 2 cups to make risotto. Use 1½ cups to make casserole. Use 2 cups to make baked penne.

YIELD: **5½** CUPS

Risotto with Sun-Dried Tomatoes and Zucchini

For perfect risotto, arborio rice is slowly simmered in hot chicken broth, and frequently stirred, until the grains are chewy and tender—or *al dente*, as they say in Italy.

Vegetable cooking spray
½ cup sun-dried tomatoes (not packed in oil)
2 cans (13¾-oz size) reduced-sodium chicken broth
1 T olive oil
2 large shallots, minced

½ cup white wine
1½ cups arborio rice
2 medium zucchini, sliced
2 cups Three-Cheese Sauce (See Master Recipe)
1 T chopped fresh parsley
½ tsp salt

SHOPPING TIP

If arborio rice is unavailable, use any medium-grain rice.

1. Line a 2-quart casserole with foil, leaving enough overhang on all sides to cover food and seal foil. Coat foil with cooking spray; set aside.

2. In small bowl, cover tomatoes with hot water; let stand 15 minutes. Drain and dice tomatoes, reserving soaking liquid.

3. In medium saucepan over high heat, combine broth and tomato-soaking liquid; bring to a boil. Reduce heat to low.

4. Warm oil in 8-quart Dutch oven over medium heat. Cook shallots about 3 minutes, until translucent, stirring. Add wine; cook about 3 minutes, or until liquid is almost all cooked off. Add rice, cook 1 minute, stirring to coat grains.

5. Add ½ cup of the simmering broth mixture; stir until liquid is absorbed. Add another ½ cup simmering broth; stir until absorbed. Continue cooking rice for about another 20 minutes, adding broth ½ cup at a time as needed and stirring often, until rice is tender, but still firm.

6. Stir in tomatoes and zucchini. Remove from heat.

7. Stir in cheese sauce, parsley, and salt.

8. Spoon into prepared casserole; cool completely before freezing.

FREEZING PLAN

• Use foil overhang to cover food and seal airtight. Freeze until solid. Remove pan; return foil package to freezer. (May also be frozen and baked in two 8- by 8-inch baking pans for smaller dinners.)

DINNER PLAN

1. Peel off foil; place risotto back into baking pan. Defrost for 2 days in refrigerator, or in microwave.

2. Preheat oven to 400°F. Bake 65 minutes, covered, or until heated through and creamy. (Baking time will vary with size of pan used.)

SERVES 6

Nutritional Information

PER SERVING: 382 cal, 16 g protein, 13 g fat, 47 g carbohydrate, 77 mg cholesterol, 956 mg sodium

Cheesy Chicken Casserole

Our shortcut version of a homey favorite starts with a roast chicken from your supermarket deli. One 2½-pound chicken yields about three cups of diced meat. The crunchy bread topping is optional; if you like, toast and prepare crumbs when making the casserole, then freeze separately.

Vegetable cooking spray
1½ cups Three-Cheese Sauce (See Master Recipe)
½ cup nonfat sour cream
1 bag (8 oz) fresh cauliflower florets, or florets from 1 small head
3 cups diced cooked chicken (from 2½-lb roasted whole chicken)
1 pkg (10 oz) frozen pearl onions, thawed and drained
1 pkg (10 oz) frozen peas, thawed
1 T chopped fresh tarragon, or 1 tsp dried
1 T chopped fresh parsley
½ tsp salt
1½ cups fresh bread cubes (from small Italian loaf) tossed with 2 T melted butter; optional topping

1. Line a 2-quart casserole with foil, leaving enough overhang on all sides to cover food and seal foil. Coat foil with cooking spray; set aside.

2. In small bowl, combine cheese sauce and sour cream.

3. Bring large saucepan of water to a boil; cook cauliflower 5 minutes, until crisp-tender. Drain; return to pot. Stir in chicken, onions, peas, tarragon, parsley, and salt, then cheese mixture. Spoon into prepared casserole; cool completely before freezing.

4. If desired, toss bread cubes with melted butter; spread in 9- by 13-inch baking pan. Bake at 400°F for 8 minutes, until crisp and golden. In food processor or blender, process cubes into medium crumbs. Cool, seal in reclosable plastic bag and freeze.

FREEZING PLAN

• Use foil overhang to cover food and seal airtight. Freeze until solid. Remove pan; return foil package to freezer. (May also be frozen and baked in two 8- by 8-inch baking pans for smaller dinners.)

DINNER PLAN

1. Peel off foil; defrost in microwave or place casserole back into baking pan and defrost for 2 days in refrigerator.

2. Preheat oven to 350°F. Bake 40 minutes, uncovered, or until heated through and bubbly. (Baking time will vary with size of pan used.)

3. If desired, top with toasted bread cubes during the last 10 minutes of cooking. Let stand 5 minutes before serving.

SERVES **6**

Nutritional Information

PER SERVING: 328 cal, 37 g protein, 12 g fat, 17 g carbohydrate, 124 mg cholesterol, 708 mg sodium

Baked Penne with Autumn Vegetables

SHOPPING TIP

Feel free to use other seasonal vegetables, such as acorn squash and plum tomatoes.

Oven roasting is a no-fuss way to cook vegetables—simply toss with oil and herbs before cooking.

Vegetable cooking spray
1 medium butternut squash (about 1¾ lb), peeled and cubed
1 pint cherry tomatoes, halved
1 large onion, cut into chunks
1 clove garlic, chopped
2 T olive oil

1 T chopped fresh thyme or 1 tsp dried
1 tsp salt
½ tsp black pepper
1 lb penne or ziti pasta
2 cups Three-Cheese Sauce (See Master Recipe)

1. Preheat oven to 400°F. Line 9- by 13-inch baking pan or oval casserole with foil, leaving enough overhang on all sides to cover food and seal foil. Coat foil with cooking spray.

2. In prepared pan, toss squash, tomatoes, onion, garlic, oil, thyme, salt, and pepper. Spread evenly; bake 30 minutes, shaking pan occasionally, until tomatoes are very soft and squash is tender but firm.

3. Meanwhile, cook pasta according to package directions about 9 minutes, or until slightly underdone. Drain; return to pasta cooking pot. Add squash mixture and cheese sauce; toss gently. Pour back into baking pan; cool completely before freezing.

FREEZING PLAN

• Use foil overhang to cover food and seal airtight. Freeze until solid. Remove pan; return foil package to freezer. (May also be frozen and baked in two 8- by 8-inch baking pans for smaller dinners.)

DINNER PLAN

1. Peel off foil; defrost in microwave or place pasta back into baking pan and defrost for 2 days in refrigerator.

2. Preheat oven to 350°F. Bake 30 minutes, covered, until heated through and bubbly.

SERVES 6 TO 8

Nutritional Information

PER SERVING: 296 cal, 14 g protein, 14 g fat, 31 g carbohydrate, 64 mg cholesterol, 613 mg sodium

Master Recipe for Roast Chicken and Garlic Pureé

For Use In: Chicken Pot Pie • Chicken Enchiladas • Chicken
Divan • Tuscan Chicken and White Bean Stew

2 whole chickens (about 6 lb each)
2 tsp salt
1 tsp black pepper
8 large heads garlic
1 T olive oil

1. Preheat oven to 450°F. Rinse chickens; pat dry. Trim off excess fat at tail and neck ends. Season cavity and outside of chicken with salt and pepper; place breast side down on racks in 2 roasting pans or 1 extra-large roasting pan.

2. Rub garlic heads with oil and place in pan alongside chickens. (If using an extra-large roasting pan, place garlic in separate small baking pan.) Roast chickens and garlic 1 hour and 10 minutes, until juices run clear when thigh is pierced with a fork. Remove chicken and garlic from oven; let cool.

3. When cool enough to handle, separate garlic into cloves; squeeze pulp out of each clove into a small bowl. Mash with a fork.

4. Remove meat from chicken and shred; discard skin and bones.

- Use 3 cups chicken for pot pie.
- Use 3 cups chicken for enchiladas.
- Use 3 cups chicken for divan.
- Use 4 cups chicken and ½ cup garlic puree for stew.
- Use ¼ cup garlic puree for garlic bread.

YIELD: ABOUT **1** CUP OF GARLIC PURÉE AND **13** CUPS OF CHICKEN MEAT

COOKING TIPS

For a perfect roast chicken every time, buy the freshest prime-quality chicken and roast at a high temperature until cooked through but still moist and juicy. Roast garlic along with chicken—the puree will keep for two weeks in the refrigerator. Use to lavishly spread on toasted bread or stir into soups and sauces.

A super-easy bonus! Great to serve alongside lasagna or ziti.

¼ cup roasted garlic puree (See Master Recipe)
2 T butter, softened
1 loaf (about 1 lb) Italian bread, split horizontally

Spread cut sides of bread with garlic puree and butter. Place halves together; wrap in foil and freeze.

 DINNER PLAN

Defrost bread, wrapped in foil, for 2 hours at room temperature. Preheat oven to 350°F. Bake foil-wrapped bread 15 to 20 minutes, until hot.

SERVES **6** TO **8**

Nutritional Information

PER SERVING: 212 cal, 7 g protein, 7 g fat, 34 g carbohydrate, 9 mg cholesterol, 420 mg sodium

Old-Fashioned Chicken Pot Pie

A substantial, heartwarming dish that makes great cold-weather eating.

FILLING
3 T butter
3 large shallots, minced
3 T flour
1 tsp dried sage
½ tsp dried thyme
1 tsp salt
½ tsp black pepper

1 cup reduced-sodium chicken broth
1 cup whole milk
1½ cups baby carrots, halved lengthwise
3 cups Roast Chicken Meat (See Master
 Recipe)
1 pkg (10 oz) mushrooms, quartered
1 cup frozen peas

1. **Line 2-quart** casserole with foil, leaving enough overhang on all sides to cover food and seal foil; set aside.

2. **Melt butter** in large deep skillet over medium-low heat. Add shallots; cook 4 minutes. Stir in flour, sage, thyme, salt, and pepper. Increase heat; add chicken broth and milk. Bring to a boil, stirring to break up any lumps of flour.

3. **Add carrots**; cook 5 minutes.

4. **Add chicken**, mushrooms, and peas; cook 5 minutes.

5. **Pour into** prepared pan. Let cool before freezing.

FREEZING PLAN

• Freeze pot-pie filling in individual size servings or all together until solid. Use foil overhang to lift frozen food from pan; cover and seal airtight. Remove pan from freezer. Return foil package to freezer.

DINNER PLAN

1. Peel off foil; defrost in microwave or place back into baking pan and defrost for 2 days in refrigerator.

2. Preheat oven to 350°F. Prepare 1 package (7½ oz) corn bread mix according to package directions. Let batter stand 5 minutes; pour over top of casserole. Bake, uncovered, 50 minutes, or until top is golden brown and filling is hot and bubbly.

MAKES **6** TO **8** SERVINGS

Nutritional Information

PER SERVING: 312 cal, 25 g protein, 12 g fat, 27 g carbohydrate, 82 mg cholesterol, 897 mg sodium

Chicken Enchiladas

1 can (15 oz) black beans, rinsed and drained
3 cups Roast Chicken Meat (See Master Recipe)
2 T chopped fresh cilantro
2 cups shredded jalapeño Jack or Monterey Jack cheese
1 jar (about 10½ oz) prepared salsa
8 large 10-inch flour tortillas
2 T olive oil

1. Line a 9- by 13-inch baking pan with foil, leaving enough overhang on all sides to cover food and seal foil; set aside.

2. In mixing bowl, combine beans, chicken, cilantro, ½ of the cheese, and ½ of the salsa.

3. For each enchilada: Rub 1 side of tortilla with oil; flip over and fill with ½ cup of chicken mixture. Roll up; place seam side down in prepared pan. Sprinkle remaining cheese over all enchiladas. (Refrigerate remaining salsa for serving.)

FREEZING PLAN

• This recipe is so versatile—you can freeze all the enchiladas together for a family dinner, or wrap separately for single servings. If freezing individually, remember to sprinkle with cheese before wrapping. If freezing together in prepared pan, freeze until solid. Use foil overhang to lift frozen food from pan; cover and seal airtight. Return package to freezer.

DINNER PLAN

1. Peel foil from enchiladas; defrost in microwave-proof pan or keep covered and defrost for 2 days in the refrigerator.

2. Preheat oven to 350°F. Place defrosted enchiladas in baking pan, cover loosely with foil; bake 20 minutes. Remove foil; bake 15 minutes more, or until heated through. Spoon remaining salsa over top of enchiladas. (Cooking time will vary with number of enchiladas.)

YIELD: **8** ENCHILADAS

Nutritional Information

PER ENCHILADA: 391 cal, 29 g protein, 17 g fat, 28 g carbohydrate, 70 mg cholesterol, 963 mg sodium

Chicken Divan

We're bringing back a favorite of the 1960s dinner table. And why not? Rich and cheesy, it's bound to be a hit with the whole family.

2 bags (8-oz size) fresh broccoli florets,
  and 1 bag (8 oz) fresh cauliflower
  florets
4 T (½ stick) butter
¼ cup all-purpose flour
1 cup reduced-sodium chicken broth
1 cup whole milk
1 cup (4 oz) shredded cheddar cheese

2 T dry sherry
1 tsp salt
½ tsp black pepper
Pinch nutmeg
3 cups Roast Chicken Meat (See Master
  Recipe)
½ cup plain dry bread crumbs

SHOPPING TIP

If your supermarket doesn't carry bags of florets, cut from whole broccoli and cauliflower heads.

1. **Line a 9- by 13-inch** baking pan or 2-quart casserole with foil, leaving enough overhang on all sides to cover food and seal foil. Butter foil; set aside.

2. **In medium saucepan**, steam broccoli and cauliflower 4 minutes over boiling water, until barely tender. Arrange in the bottom of prepared pan.

3. **Melt butter** in medium saucepan over medium heat. Add flour; cook 2 minutes, until light brown, stirring constantly with a whisk or fork. Whisk in broth and milk; cook about 5 minutes, or until sauce thickens, stirring frequently. Remove from heat; stir in ¼ cup of the cheese. Add sherry, salt, pepper, and nutmeg.

4. **Pour ½ of the sauce** over broccoli and cauliflower. Sprinkle chicken over sauce. Top with remaining sauce, then remaining cheese and bread crumbs. Let cool before freezing.

FREEZING PLAN

• Freeze divan until solid. Use foil overhang to lift frozen food from pan; cover and seal airtight. Return foil packet to freezer. (May also be frozen and baked in two 8- by 8-inch baking pans for smaller dinners.)

DINNER PLAN

1. Peel foil from divan; defrost in microwave; or place back into baking pan and defrost in refrigerator for 2 days.

2. Preheat oven to 350°F. Bake 30 minutes, uncovered, or until heated through. (Baking time will vary with size of pan used.)

MAKES 6 TO 8 SERVINGS

Nutritional Information

PER SERVING: 326 cal, 28 g protein, 17 g fat, 16 g carbohydrate, 91 mg cholesterol, 856 mg sodium

Tuscan Chicken and White Bean Stew

This rich and warming stew, fragrant with garlic and rosemary, is the perfect meal for a chilly autumn evening. If this much garlic or rosemary seems too strong for your kids, use half the amount given.

½ cup roasted garlic puree (see Roast Chicken recipe, page 77)

4 cans (15-oz size) cannellini (or Great Northern) beans, drained and rinsed

2 cans (13¾-oz size) reduced-sodium chicken broth

¼ lb pancetta or bacon, diced

1 cup thinly sliced baby carrots

2 large shallots, minced

½ cup white wine or water

1 T chopped fresh rosemary or 2 tsp dried

4 cups Roast Chicken Meat (See Master Recipe)

½ tsp salt

½ tsp black pepper

1. In blender, puree 2 cups of the beans and 1 cup of the chicken broth with garlic puree; set aside.

2. In 5-quart pot over medium heat, cook pancetta 4 minutes until browned, stirring often. Add carrots and shallots; cook 2 minutes longer, stirring. Add wine and rosemary; bring to a boil and simmer, uncovered, 3 minutes.

3. Stir in pureed bean mixture, remaining broth, remaining whole beans, and chicken. Increase heat to medium-high. Bring mixture to a boil; simmer, uncovered, 5 minutes. Stir in salt and pepper.

FREEZING PLAN

• May be frozen in any size plastic container for single-serve or family dinners.

DINNER PLAN

Defrost for 2 days in the refrigerator, or in microwave. Reheat in microwave or transfer to saucepan and simmer gently over low heat until heated through.

MAKES **6** TO **8** SERVINGS

Nutritional Information

PER SERVING: 395 cal, 42 g protein, 11 g fat, 41 g carbohydrate, 73 mg cholesterol, 793 mg sodium

Master Recipe for Tomato Meat Sauce

For Use in: Tex-Mex Chili • Lasagna • Pizza • Baked Ziti

1 T olive oil
2 large onions, coarsely chopped
4 cloves garlic, minced
2 lb lean ground beef
6 cans (28-oz size) plum tomatoes, with juice
1 can (6 oz) tomato paste
½ cup chopped fresh parsley (or 2 T dried)

½ cup chopped fresh basil (or 2 T dried)
3 bay leaves
1 T granulated sugar
1½ tsp salt
1½ tsp black pepper

COOKING TIPS

To save time, do all the prep work while the sauce is simmering. If you have sauce left over after preparing all recipes, freeze it to use as a quick topping for pasta.

1. Warm olive oil in an 8-quart pot over medium heat. Add onions; cook 8 minutes. Add garlic; cook 1 minute, stirring often.

2. Increase heat; add beef and cook until browned, stirring often.

3. Add remaining ingredients; bring to a simmer. Reduce heat to low; simmer 2 hours, stirring occasionally and breaking up tomatoes with a wooden spoon.

* Use 5 cups for chili.

* Use 6 cups for lasagna.

* Use 2 cups for pizza.

* Use 6 cups for baked ziti.

YIELD: ABOUT **22** CUPS

Tex-Mex Chili

Everybody loves chili! This one is moderately spicy—if you like it more fiery, add another jalapeño pepper and a touch more chili powder. Top with grated cheddar cheese and additional chopped fresh cilantro, if desired.

1 lb reduced-sodium bacon
1 green bell pepper, seeded and diced
1 large onion, diced
1 jalapeño pepper, seeded and minced
¼ cup chopped fresh cilantro
2 tsp chili powder
1 tsp ground cumin
5 cups Tomato Meat Sauce (see Master Recipes)
2 cans (15-oz size) red kidney beans, rinsed and drained

1. In 8-quart pot over low heat, cook bacon until crisp. Drain on paper towels, then crumble.

2. Discard all but 1 tablespoon of the drippings from pan. To drippings, add green pepper and onion; cook over medium heat 5 minutes, or until softened. Add jalapeño pepper, cilantro, chili powder, and cumin; cook 2 minutes, stirring.

3. Remove from heat; stir in bacon, Master Sauce, and beans. Let cool before freezing.

FREEZING PLAN

• May be frozen in any size plastic container for single-serve or family dinners.

DINNER PLAN

Defrost in microwave or for 2 days in the refrigerator. Reheat in microwave or transfer to saucepan and simmer gently over low heat until heated through.

MAKES **6** TO **8** SERVINGS

Nutritional Information

PER SERVING: 293 cal, 19 g protein, 15 g fat, 22 g carbohydrate, 40 mg cholesterol, 746 mg sodium

Classic—but Quick—Lasagna

Lasagna is the perfect dish to go from freezer to oven to table. The noodles need no precooking—the moisture from freezing is sufficient to cook them during the baking. A terrific timesaver!

1 container (15 oz) part-skim ricotta cheese
2 large eggs
½ cup grated Parmesan cheese
¼ cup chopped fresh parsley
2 tsp dried oregano
6 cups Tomato Meat Sauce (See Master Recipe)
1 lb uncooked lasagna noodles (about 15 noodles)
1½ cups (6 oz) shredded mozzarella cheese

1. In medium bowl, combine first 5 ingredients; set aside.

2. Line a 9- by 13-inch baking pan with foil, leaving enough overhang on all sides to cover food and seal foil. Spread 1 cup of the Master Sauce in the bottom of pan. Cover with 5 of the dry lasagna noodles, ⅓ of the remaining Master Sauce, and 1 cup of the ricotta mixture. Then layer with 5 more noodles, ⅓ of the remaining Master Sauce, and the remaining 1 cup of ricotta mixture. Top with final 5 noodles and remaining Master Sauce. Sprinkle with mozzarella.

FREEZING PLAN

• Freeze lasagna until solid. Use foil overhang to lift frozen food from pan; cover and seal airtight. Return foil packet to freezer.

DINNER PLAN

1. Preheat oven to 350°F. Peel foil from lasagna; place back into baking pan.

2. Cover loosely with foil; bake frozen (not defrosted) lasagna 45 minutes.

3. Remove foil; bake 30 minutes longer, or until hot and bubbly. Allow to set 10 minutes before cutting.

MAKES **6** TO **8** SERVINGS

Nutritional Information

PER SERVING: 441 cal, 34 g protein, 21 g fat, 29 g carbohydrate, 135 mg cholesterol, 705 mg sodium

Family-Style Pizza

This recipe makes two entirely different pizzas—one "plain" for finicky eaters, and one loaded with the works. Since you don't need to defrost before baking, they make a great last-minute supper.

2 pkg (10-oz size) refrigerated pizza dough
2 cups Tomato Meat Sauce (See Master Recipe)

FOR THE KIDS
½ cup shredded mozzarella cheese

WITH THE WORKS
½ cup shredded mozzarella cheese
18 slices pepperoni
1 green bell pepper, seeded and thinly sliced
¼ cup marinated artichoke hearts

1. Line 2 baking sheets with foil, leaving enough overhang on all sides to cover food and seal foil; set aside. On a clean surface, unroll both pizza doughs. Form dough into 2 pizza crusts; place on prepared pans.

2. Spread each crust with 1 cup Master Sauce, then top each with ½ cup mozzarella cheese. Top 1 pizza with remaining toppings.

FREEZING PLAN

- Cool pizza completely. Freeze covered in foil.

DINNER PLAN

1. Preheat oven to 450°F. Peel foil from pizzas; place on greased baking sheet.

2. Bake frozen (not defrosted) pizzas 15 to 25 minutes, or until crusts are browned and cheese melts.

MAKES **6** TO **8** SERVINGS

Nutritional Information

PER SERVING: 289 cal, 15 g protein, 8 g fat, 40 g carbohydrate, 18 mg cholesterol, 635 mg sodium

Baked Ziti with 4 Cheeses

The preshredded 4-cheese mix (a blend of Parmesan, mozzarella, ricotta, and provolone) is available at most supermarkets.

1 lb ziti or penne pasta
6 cups Tomato Meat Sauce (See Master Recipe)
4 cups (1 lb) shredded 4-cheese blend, or shredded mozzarella cheese

1. Line a 9- by 13-inch baking pan with foil, leaving enough overhang on all sides to cover food and seal foil; set aside.

2. Cook ziti in boiling water 5 minutes, until tender but not quite done; drain.

3. In large bowl, combine ziti, Master Sauce, and ½ of the cheese. Turn into prepared pan. Top with remaining cheese. Let cool before freezing.

FREEZING PLAN

• Freeze ziti until solid. Use foil overhang to lift frozen food from pan; cover and seal airtight. Return foil package to freezer. (May also be frozen in any size plastic container for single-serve or smaller dinners.)

DINING PLAN

1. Peel foil from ziti; defrost in microwave or place, covered, back into baking pan and defrost for 2 days in refrigerator.

2. Preheat oven to 350°F. Cover loosely with foil; bake 15 minutes. Remove foil; bake 30 minutes longer, until hot and bubbly.

MAKES **6** TO **8** SERVINGS

Nutritional Information

PER SERVING: 372 cal, 29 g protein, 17 g fat, 26 g carbohydrate, 66 mg cholesterol, 617 mg sodium

7-Day Dinner Plans

•   •   •

How the 7-Day Menus Work

One-shop, cook-ahead, interlocking menus make these 7-day dinner plans easy to follow, and they save you an enormous amount of time and hassles throughout the week.

We've organized 8 weeks' worth of dinner plans. The menus begin on Saturday and take you through Friday.

Each week contains interlocking recipes that, in effect, leverage a weekend's worth of cooking into a week's worth of quick dinners. The trick is that you cook larger quantities on the weekend. This extra food becomes the building blocks for dinner on busy weeknights. As long as the grill is going for Saturday's salmon, why not grill some chicken for a future night? Then, the rest of the week, the hard part is already done for you—no need to plan or shop, just take out what's already in your refrigerator, and transform it into dinner. The best part is that the weeknight meals will taste different and unique. They won't seem like leftovers at all.

How to Build the Week's Meals

Before you start on any of the 7-day dinner plans, keep in mind the following points:

1. Menus make use of the most perishable items first and call for ingredients more than once, so you don't end up with a refrigerator full of spoiled produce. The cooking and eating schedule should be followed as much as possible, because of the perishablility of some of the ingredients. For example, fresh fish is best cooked the day purchased, and cooked fish should be used within 2 days.

2. To avoid rush-hour trips to the market, all shopping is done on Saturday for the entire week, using our easy-to-follow shopping list. Desserts aren't included, so add your family's favorites. Because meats and salad greens don't store well for an entire week, Friday's meal is usually rather light. If you have some hearty eaters at home, you may wish to supplement with other foods on that night.

3. Be sure to read the timesaving-strategies box following recipes—these let you know what to make ahead or save for a later meal.

All cooked food should be tightly wrapped and refrigerated. Fresh herbs should be wrapped in damp paper towels and refrigerated in plastic bags. Store precleaned salad greens in the specially designed bags in which you purchased them—and don't open them until you need to.

If bread is not to be used until later in the week, it should be frozen in a re-sealable plastic bag, defrosted at room temperature, then reheated before eating. Detailed storing and reheating instructions can be found in the timesaving-strategies box.

4. If you must skip a weeknight meal, most of the ingredients will be fine for the next day, without an appreciable loss in quality. After two days, however, it would be a smart idea to make the dish anyway, and eat it for lunch, or give it to a friend. Note, however, that some of the meals can be frozen—we've indicated those that can.

• • •

Seared Basil Sea Scallops with Emerald Orzo (p. 4)

. . .

Mashed Potato Salad (p. 11)

• • •

Three-Pea Creamy Pasta Salad (p.22)

• • •

Garlicky Shrimp and Swiss Chard (p.26)

Seared Salmon with Caramelized Carrots and Onions (p.32)

• • •

Dijon Pork Chops (p. 36)

• • •

Chicken Tortilla Soup (p. 46)

• • •

Meatballs and ABCs (p.48)

• • •

North Carolina Pulled Pork Sandwich (p. 65)

· · ·

Spicy Chorizo Chili (p.66)

Baked Penne with
Autumn Vegetables (p. 75)

All-American BBQ Chicken (left); Grilled
Summer Squash (right) (p. 105); Texas
Charred-Chicken Salad (front) (p. 111)

• • •

Middle Eastern Grilled Steak, Chickpea Salad with Lime Dressing and
Cucumber Riata; (left) (p.101); Warm steak and Couscous with Cucumber
Salsa (right) (p.109); Golden Corn Chowder (back) (p.108)

• • •

Hot Brisket Sandwiches with Caramelized Onions (p. 143)

. . .

Chicken Curry with Potatoes and Green Beans (p.144)

· · ·

Braised Beef Brisket with Roasted Vegetables (p. 135)

Grill It!

This week's menu starts with a grilled steak accompanied by a cucumber salad and a chickpea dish. On Sunday enjoy BBQ chicken and corn on the cob with grilled squash. Save half the recipe for Wednesday's pasta, and some of the chicken for Tuesday's chicken salad. Extra cooked corn makes a rich chowder on Thursday. Friday's meal is a restaurant-style layered bean dip and juicy grilled hamburgers.

MENU

Saturday
Middle Eastern Grilled Steak
Cucumber Riata and Chickpea Salad with Lime Dressing
Grilled Pita Rounds

Sunday
All-American BBQ Chicken
Grilled Summer Squash
Corn on the Cob

Monday
Warm Steak and Couscous with Cucumber Salsa
Pita Crisps with Homemade Hummus

Tuesday
Texas Charred-Chicken Salad
Tortilla Chips

Wednesday
Ziti with Squash and Feta
Green Salad
Warm French Baguette

Thursday
Bacon, Guacamole, and Tomato Sandwiches
Golden Corn Chowder

Friday
Grilled Basic Burgers
Amazing Seven-Layer Dip and Chips

Produce
3 large limes
1 bag (10 oz) precleaned salad
  greens, preferably Romaine blend
1 bunch scallions
1 bunch fresh Italian parsley
1 large bunch fresh thyme
1 bunch fresh cilantro
4 medium cucumbers
6 large tomatoes
4 medium zucchini
4 medium yellow squash
10 ears fresh corn
1 large red pepper
1 medium Yukon gold or all-
  purpose potato
1 small red onion
2 small yellow onions
1 head garlic

Meat
2 lb ground beef
3¼ lb top round or London broil
  steak, about 1½ inches thick
5 lb chicken pieces (1 whole
  chicken, cut up, plus 4 breast
  halves)
½ lb bacon slices
1 box (12 oz) ziti or penne pasta

Canned/Packaged
1 pkg (about 6 oz) curry-flavored
  couscous mix
1 small jar (8 oz) tahini (sesame
  paste)
2 cans (19-oz size) chickpeas
1 can (15 oz) black beans
1 can (16 oz) low-fat refried beans
1 bag (10–16 oz) tortilla chips

1 container (16 oz) prepared guacamole
1 jar (8 oz) prepared salsa

Dairy
1 container (8 oz) nonfat plain yogurt
1 container (8 oz) reduced-fat sour
  cream
1 carton (8 oz) half-and-half
1 bag (8 oz) shredded cheddar cheese
1 pkg (8 oz) feta cheese

Bread
1 pkg (16 oz) large pita rounds
  (You'll need 8.)
2 French baguettes (about 12 inches
  in length)
1 pkg hamburger buns (You'll need 4.)

Staples
Olive oil
Cider vinegar
White-wine vinegar (You'll need
  about ½ cup.)
Hot pepper sauce
Worcestershire sauce
Ketchup
Granulated sugar
Ground cinnamon
Ground cumin
Paprika
Cayenne pepper
Salt and black pepper
Aluminum foil, resealable plastic
  bags, plastic wrap

Desserts
Your choice!

Saturday's Dinner: Middle Eastern Grilled Steak with Cucumber Riata, Chickpea Salad with Lime Dressing, and Grilled Pita Rounds

SERVES 4

Middle Eastern Grilled Steak

We like this steak well-seared on the outside, so make sure your fire is hot.

2 T olive oil
2 tsp fresh thyme or 1 tsp dried
½ tsp ground cumin
½ tsp ground cinnamon
½ tsp paprika
½ tsp salt
¼ tsp black pepper
3¼ lb top round or London broil steak, about 1½-inches thick

1. Preheat grill to high. Position oiled grill rack at least 4 inches from coals.

2. In small bowl, combine first 7 ingredients. Rub on both sides of steak.

3. Grill 5 minutes per side, until dark brown and crusty on the outside and medium rare on the inside. Place pita on edge of grill to warm.

4. Slice off ⅓ of the steak (about 1 lb); reserve for later use. Slice and serve remaining steak.

Cucumber Riata

This light, cool salad is a perfect accompaniment to the hearty steak.

3 medium cucumbers, peeled
1 container (8 oz) plain nonfat yogurt
¼ cup chopped fresh Italian parsley
2 scallions, thinly sliced
1 T fresh lime juice
1 T olive oil
1 clove garlic, minced
½ tsp salt

1. Halve cucumbers lengthwise. With a teaspoon, scoop out seeds, then cut into thin slices.

2. In medium serving bowl, combine remaining ingredients. Mix in cucumber. Reserve 1½ cups for later use. Serve remaining salad chilled.

Chickpea Salad with Lime Dressing

Also known as garbanzos, chickpeas are a rich source of protein, B vitamins, and fiber. The salad may be served chilled or at room temperature. Reserve some of it to make hummus for Monday.

LIME DRESSING
6 T olive oil
¼ cup white-wine vinegar
1 tsp lime peel
¼ cup fresh lime juice
¼ cup fresh Italian parsley
3 cloves garlic, minced

½ tsp salt
¼ tsp black pepper (optional)

SALAD
2 cans (19-oz size) chickpeas, rinsed
*   and drained*
½ small red onion, chopped

1. For dressing: In small jar with tight-fitting lid, shake all ingredients until well blended.

2. In large serving bowl, toss ½ of dressing (about ½ cup) with salad ingredients. Reserve remaining dressing for later use. Reserve 1½ cups salad for later use; serve remaining salad.

 TIMESAVING STRATEGIES

- When reserved steak is cool, wrap well and refrigerate to use Monday.

- Refrigerate remaining ½ cup Lime Dressing to use Tuesday.

- Refrigerate 1½ cup chickpea salad and make hummus (recipe follows). Refrigerate hummus to use Monday.

- Refrigerate reserved 1½ cup riata to use Monday.

- Refrigerate ½ red onion to use Sunday.

- Reserve remaining pita rounds, at room temperature, to use Monday.

- Assemble hamburgers (recipe follows); freeze to use Friday.

- Freeze hamburger buns and 2 baguettes (see grocery list) in re-sealable plastic bags to use Wednesday, Thursday, and Friday.

Nutritional Information

PER SERVING OF STEAK: 224 cal, 36 g protein, 8 g fat, trace carbohydrate, 95 mg cholesterol, 158 mg sodium
PER SERVING OF CHICKPEAS: 198 cal, 8 g protein, 7 g fat, 26 g carbohydrate, 0 mg cholesterol, 141 mg sodium
PER SERVING OF RIATA: 76 cal, 4 g protein, 3 g fat, 9 g carbohydrate, 1 mg cholesterol, 253 mg sodium

Homemade-Ahead Hummus

Hummus takes only 5 minutes to make, and it's great to have in your fridge to use as a healthy dip or sandwich spread. You'll have leftover tahini (sesame paste), so next time you want to make hummus, just substitute drained, canned chickpeas for the chickpea salad.

1½ cups chickpea salad (reserved from above)
¾ cup tahini (sesame paste)
¼ cup chopped fresh Italian parsley
1 T fresh lime juice
½ tsp salt

In a food processor fitted with metal blade, process all ingredients and ½ cup water until well combined. Transfer to an airtight container. Store, covered, in the refrigerator.

Do-Ahead Basic Burgers

Take a few moments tonight and assemble burgers for Friday night. Quickly and lightly mix and form the meat—overmixing will make the burgers dense and heavy.

2 lb ground beef
½ tsp hot pepper sauce
½ tsp Worcestershire sauce
¼ tsp salt
¼ tsp pepper

1. **In a medium mixing bowl,** combine all ingredients. Gently form into 4 to 6 patties (depending on your family's appetite), about ¾-inch thick.

2. **Wrap individually in plastic wrap,** then in foil. Freeze until Thursday night for Friday's dinner.

Sunday's Dinner: All-American BBQ Chicken with
Grilled Summer Squash and Corn on the Cob
— SERVES 4 —

All-American BBQ Chicken

The BBQ sauce is very mild (we made it with kids in mind)—increase the hot pepper sauce if you like. You could also use a prepared BBQ sauce. Buy whatever chicken parts your family likes, but be sure to include some meaty breasts that will be reserved for Wednesday's chicken salad.

BBQ SAUCE
1 T olive oil
1 small yellow onion, chopped
1 cup ketchup
¼ cup cider vinegar
3 T Worcestershire sauce
1 T granulated sugar
1 tsp hot pepper sauce
1 tsp salt

CHICKEN
5 lb chicken pieces (about 10 pieces)
2 T olive oil
1 tsp salt
½ tsp black pepper

1. For sauce: Warm oil in large skillet over medium heat. Cook onion about 5 minutes, stirring. Add all remaining sauce ingredients; reduce heat and simmer, partially covered, about 20 minutes, or until flavors blend, stirring occasionally. Set aside.

2. Preheat grill to medium-high. Rinse and pat dry chicken; rub with oil, covering all surfaces, then sprinkle with salt and pepper. Grill chicken 15 minutes, turning. Baste thoroughly on both sides with sauce. Grill 5 minutes more, until cooked through. Chicken is done when meat near the bone is no longer pink.

3. Reserve 3 large pieces chicken (about 1¼ lb) for later use. Serve remaining chicken.

Grilled Summer Squash

Here, the light vinaigrette doubles as a marinade and a dressing. After all the squash is grilled, toss it with any remaining marinade to add moisture and flavor. If you have one, grill the squash in a vegetable basket.

¼ cup olive oil
2 T white-wine vinegar
½ tsp salt
¼ tsp black pepper
4 medium zucchini, thickly sliced
4 medium yellow squash, thickly sliced

1. In large bowl, combine first 4 ingredients. Marinate squash slices in mixture for 10 minutes.

2. Grill, alongside chicken, 2 to 4 minutes per side, until lightly browned, using tongs to turn squash.

3. In a medium serving bowl, toss grilled squash with enough marinade to moisten. Reserve half of mixture (about 3 cups, plus any remaining marinade) for later use. Serve remaining squash hot or at room temperature.

Corn on the Cob

Unlike most veggies, corn gets tougher, not softer, when cooked too long. The freshest ears take only 3 minutes in boiling water. Saving the corn cooking water for Thursday's chowder is not imperative, but it does add to chowder's flavor.

10 ears fresh corn

1. Bring a large pot of water to a boil. Add 10 ears fresh, shucked corn; cook 3 to 5 minutes, until just tender. Drain; reserving 6 ears cooked corn for later use.

2. Serve remaining ears with butter, salt, and pepper, if desired. Reserve 5 cups corn cooking water for later use.

TIMESAVING STRATEGIES

- Refrigerate reserved 3 cups squash and any marinade left in bowl to use Wednesday.

- When reserved chicken is cool, wrap well and refrigerate to use Tuesday.

- Scrape kernels from 6 reserved ears corn. Make corn chowder (recipe follows), using 2 cups of the kernels and 5 cups of the corn cooking water. Reserve an additional 1 cup corn kernels to use Wednesday.

- Reserve remaining ½ red pepper (used in corn chowder) to use Monday.

Nutritional Information

PER SERVING OF CHICKEN: 261 cal, 22 g protein, 14 g fat, 14 g carbohydrate, 65 mg cholesterol, 1150 mg sodium

PER SERVING OF SQUASH: 76 cal, 1 g protein, 7 g fat, 4 g carbohydrate, 0 mg cholesterol, 137 mg sodium

PER EAR OF CORN: 80 cal, 3 g protein, 1 g fat, 18 g carbohydrate, 0 mg cholesterol, 10 mg sodium

Do-Ahead Golden Corn Chowder

Start this summertime classic tonight—it will take just minutes to finish on Thursday. To save time on Monday, dice the whole red pepper while making the chowder, and wrap half of the cubes in plastic.

2 T olive oil
1 medium Yukon Gold or all-purpose potato, peeled and cut into small dice
½ small red onion, chopped
½ large red pepper, cut into small dice
2 tsp fresh thyme, or 1 tsp dried
5 cups corn cooking water (reserved from Sunday)
1 tsp salt
¼ tsp black pepper
Pinch cayenne pepper, optional
2 cups corn kernels (reserved from Sunday)

1. Warm oil in large pot over medium-low heat. Cook potato, onion, red pepper, and thyme 10 minutes, until softened, stirring.

2. Add corn broth, salt, black pepper, and cayenne. Increase heat; bring just to a boil. Reduce heat and simmer about 10 minutes.

3. Remove from heat, stir in corn kernels. Refrigerate, tightly covered, to finish Thursday.

Warm Steak and Couscous with Cucumber Salsa

We like a curry couscous here, but you may substitute plain couscous for picky eaters. Any leftover hummus will keep, tightly covered, in your refrigerator for up to a week. For a nutritious workday lunch, bring to the office along with celery and baby carrots for dipping.

1 pkg (about 6 oz) curry-flavored couscous mix
1 T olive oil
½ red pepper, diced (reserved from Sunday)
1 lb grilled steak (reserved from Saturday), thinly sliced
1½ cup riata (reserved from Saturday)
1 medium tomato, coarsely chopped
¼ cup fresh Italian parsley, chopped
½ pkg (8-oz size) feta cheese, crumbled

1. Cook couscous according to package directions.

2. Warm oil in medium skillet over low heat. Cook red pepper 5 minutes, until softened, stirring. Add steak slices; warm over low heat about 5 minutes, stirring.

3. In small serving bowl, combine riata, tomato, and parsley; sprinkle with feta. To serve: Pile couscous on plate; top with meat and pepper mixture and cucumber salsa.

Homemade Hummus with Pita Crisps

4 pita rounds

1. Cut pita rounds into quarters; warm in toaster oven if desired.

2. Serve with Homemade Hummus (reserved from Sunday) for dipping.

 TIMESAVING STRATEGIES

- Reserve remaining half package of feta cheese to use Thursday.

Nutritional Information

PER SERVING OF COUSCOUS: 445 cal, 46 g protein, 19 g fat, 34 g carbohydrate, 119 mg cholesterol, 570 mg sodium

PER SERVING OF HUMMUS: 205 cal, 7 g protein, 15 g fat, 13 g carbohydrate, 0 mg cholesterol, 190 mg sodium

Texas Charred-Chicken Salad

Use a crunchy, Romaine-based salad blend for this colorful dish. Serve with half a bag tortilla chips for dipping.

1¼ lb BBQ chicken (reserved from Sunday)
1 can (15 oz) black beans, drained and rinsed
2 large tomatoes, chopped
1 cup corn kernels (reserved from Sunday)
½ cup Lime Dressing (reserved from Saturday)
½ tsp ground cumin
¼ tsp salt
½ pkg (10-oz size) precleaned salad greens—preferably Romaine
2 T chopped fresh cilantro, optional

1. Pull chicken from bone; cut into bite-sized chunks.

2. In large serving bowl, combine chicken, beans, tomatoes, and corn.

3. Toss with dressing, cumin, and salt. Serve over lettuce; sprinkle with cilantro, if desired.

 TIMESAVING STRATEGIES

- Reserve half of the bag of tortilla chips to use Friday.
- Refrigerate remaining half bag of salad greens to use Wednesday.
- Remove one baguette from freezer Wednesday morning; defrost, in resealable bag, at room temperature.

Nutritional Information

PER SERVING: 385 cal, 23 g protein, 20 g fat, 33 g carbohydrate, 53 mg cholesterol, 1179 mg sodium

Ziti with Squash and Feta

To round out the meal, toss the remaining half a bag of salad greens with your favorite prepared greens. Warm the bread while the pasta cooks.

1 box (12 oz) ziti or penne pasta
1 T olive oil
1 small onion, chopped
1 clove garlic, chopped
2 tsp fresh thyme, or 1 tsp dried

3 cups grilled squash (reserved from Saturday), plus marinade in bowl
½ tsp salt
¼ tsp black pepper
½ pkg (8-oz size) feta cheese, crumbled

1. Cook pasta according to package directions; drain.

2. Warm oil in large skillet over medium-low heat. Cook onion, garlic, and thyme 5 minutes, until vegetables soften, stirring. Add squash and marinade, salt and pepper; cook about 7 minutes, until warmed through. In large serving bowl, toss sauce with pasta and cheese.

TIMESAVING STRATEGIES

- Remove remaining baguette from freezer on Thursday morning; defrost, in resealable bag, at room temperature.

Nutritional Information

PER SERVING: 308 cal, 10 g protein, 17 g fat, 31 g carbohydrate, 25 mg cholesterol, 720 mg sodium

Bacon, Guacamole, and Tomato Sandwiches

Sandwiches are always a good choice for a fast, cool summer dinner. We used a French baguette here, but feel free to substitute your family's favorite bread.

½ lb bacon slices
1 long French baguette (about 12 inches in length), cut into 4 pieces
½ cup prepared guacamole
2 large tomatoes, cut into 8 thick slices
1 medium cucumber, peeled and thinly sliced

1. In large skillet over medium heat, cook bacon slices until crisp. Remove to paper towels.

2. Meanwhile, slice each bread piece horizontally to make 4 sandwiches. Lightly toast in toaster oven or broiler. Layer each sandwich with guacamole, bacon slices, tomato, and cucumber.

Golden Corn Chowder

If you like, you can save some of the bacon from the sandwiches to sprinkle over the chowder. This recipe makes plenty for a family of 4—save some for tomorrow's lunch, if you like.

Corn chowder (reserved from Sunday)
1 carton (8 oz) half-and-half
⅓ cup reduced-fat sour cream, optional
2 T chopped fresh cilantro, optional

In medium saucepan over medium-low heat, bring chowder to a gentle simmer, then stir in half-and-half. Once you've added the cream, don't let the soup boil. Garnish with sour cream and cilantro, if desired.

TIMESAVING STRATEGIES

- Remove hamburgers from freezer; defrost, still wrapped, in refrigerator to use Friday.

- Refrigerate remaining guacamole to use Friday.

- Remove hamburger buns from freezer on Friday morning; defrost, in resealable bag, at room temperature.

Nutritional Information

PER SERVING OF SANDWICH: 423 cal, 15 g protein, 20 g fat, 48 g carbohydrate, 16 mg cholesterol, 1150 mg sodium

PER SERVING OF CHOWDER: 294 cal, 13 g protein, 18 g fat, 21 g carbohydrate, 34 mg cholesterol, 961 mg sodium

Grilled Basic Burgers

The juiciest hamburgers are made from chuck, or 80 to 85 percent lean beef.

4 burgers (formed and frozen on Sunday)
4 hamburger buns, split
1 cup shredded cheddar cheese, optional

1. Preheat grill to medium. Grill patties for 6 minutes per side, or until desired doneness.

2. Sprinkle with cheese in last minute of grilling, if desired. Toast buns by placing them, split side down, on edge of grill until lightly browned.

Amazing 7-Layer Dip

Serve our version of this restaurant favorite with the remaining half bag of tortilla chips.

⅔ cup reduced-fat sour cream
¼ tsp ground cumin
Pinch salt
1 can (16 oz) low-fat refried beans
1 cup shredded cheddar cheese
½ cup prepared guacamole (reserved from Thursday)
½ cup prepared salsa
2 scallions, thinly sliced
1 T chopped fresh cilantro

COOKING TIP

Don't press down on the patty when grilling, it will squeeze out the flavorful juices and may cause a flare-up.

1. In small bowl, combine first 3 ingredients. Set aside.

2. In small saucepan over medium-low heat, warm beans. Spread warm beans in the center of a shallow 8-inch serving platter. Sprinkle half of the cheese over beans. Top with guacamole, salsa, sour cream mixture, scallions, the remaining half of the cheese, and cilantro. Serve with chips and extra salsa, if desired.

Nutritional Information

PER SERVING OF BURGERS: 492 cal, 50 g protein, 31 g fat, 0 g carbohydrate, 178 mg cholesterol, 290 mg sodium

PER SERVING OF DIP: 294 cal, 13 g protein, 18 g fat, 21 g carbohydrate, 34 mg cholesterol, 961 mg sodium

Comfort Food Plus

Here is a week of streamlined classic dishes. Start with a simple chicken stew. Save some of the braised meat for a chicken salad on Tuesday. Sunday's dinner is homemade pub food—fish and chips. Take some time to make a rich tomato meat sauce that's used in Monday's pasta and in Thursday's burrito.

Wednesday is comfort-food hash, made with Sunday's leftover baked potatoes. Friday's meal is easiest of all—a hearty layered sandwich.

MENU

Saturday
Chicken Fricassee with Egg Noodles

Sunday
Fish and Chips
Peas

Monday
Spaghetti Bolognese
Green Salad
Garlic Bread

Tuesday
Balsamic Chicken Caesar Salad
Walnut Bread

Wednesday
Virginia Ham Hash with Applesauce
Toast

Thursday
Burrito Grande
Spanish Rice

Friday
Muffuletta
Iceberg Salad
Fresh Fruit

•   •   •

GROCERY LIST FOR THE WEEK

Produce
2 large Spanish onions
1 head garlic
1 bunch celery
1 bunch fresh thyme
1 lb carrots
1 small head iceberg lettuce
1 bag (10 oz) lettuce
1 small head Romaine lettuce
1 lemon
8 large russet potatoes
5 plum tomatoes
1 jalapeño pepper

Dairy
1 carton (8 oz) half-and-half
Butter (4 T)
1 block (4 oz) Parmesan cheese
1 container (8 oz) nonfat plain yogurt
Large eggs (4)
1 bag (8 oz) shredded Monterey Jack cheese
Large flour tortillas (6)
½ lb provolone or fontina cheese, sliced

Packaged Goods
1 box (about 6 oz) Spanish or other rice mix
2 cans (13¾-oz size) reduced-sodium chicken broth
1 box (8 oz) egg noodles
1 can (28 oz) whole tomatoes
1 can (15 oz) tomato sauce
1 box (12 oz) spaghetti or fettucine
1 small tube anchovy paste
1 jar (12 oz) gardineria (pepper and olive salad)
1 jar (16 oz) favorite applesauce

Frozen
1 pkg (10 oz) frozen corn
1 pkg (10 oz) frozen peas
1 pkg (10 oz) frozen garlic bread

Meat/Fish
5 lb bone-in chicken pieces (1 whole fryer chicken plus 4 breast halves)
4 thin fish fillets (about 4 oz each), such as sole, flounder, or trout
½ lb sweet Italian sausage (2 small links)
1 lb lean ground beef
12 oz Virginia or Black Forest ham, thinly sliced
½ lb spicy or sweet salami, sliced

Bakery
4 bakery whole-wheat walnut rolls
1 round loaf Italian or peasant bread loaf (about 8 inches in diameter)
1 loaf favorite sliced bread

Staples
Olive oil
Prepared salad dressing
Dried bay leaves
All-purpose flour
Ground cumin
Chili powder
Salt and black pepper
Balsamic vinegar
Aluminum foil, large resealable plastic bags, plastic wrap

Miscellaneous
White wine (good enough to drink)

Chicken Fricassee

The preparation of the sauce for this dish involves lots of chopping, but this medley of sautéed vegetables, also called a *mirepoix,* provides the base for three future meals. If you have a food processor, let it do the chopping for you. Keep an eye on the simmering; you want to maintain enough liquid to ensure moistness. Add more broth or water if chicken appears to be drying out. Cook up an 8 oz bag of egg noodles to soak up the sauce. If you like, have a glass of wine with dinner, but reserve ¾ cup to use Sunday.

2 T olive oil
5 lb bone-in chicken pieces (1 whole
  fryer chicken plus 4 breast halves)
1 tsp salt
6 celery stalks, thinly sliced
1 lb carrots, thinly sliced
2 large Spanish onions, thinly sliced
2 garlic cloves, thinly sliced

2 tsp fresh thyme or 1 tsp dried
2 bay leaves
¼ cup all-purpose flour
1 cup dry white wine
1 can (13¾ oz) plus ¾ cup reduced-
  sodium chicken broth
½ cup half-and-half
½ pkg (10-oz size) frozen corn, thawed

1. Warm oil in large Dutch oven over medium-high heat. Meanwhile, wash and pat dry chicken; sprinkle with salt. Brown chicken in 3 batches until browned on both sides, about 4 minutes per side, turning with tongs. Set aside.

2. In same pot over medium heat, cook celery, carrots, onion, garlic, thyme, and bay leaves about 15 minutes, until vegetables soften, stirring to loosen browned bits. Remove half of the mixture (about 3 cups), reserve for later use. Sprinkle flour over vegetables remaining in pot, stirring constantly.

3. When flour is completely incorporated, gradually add wine, broth, and browned chicken; bring to a simmer. Partially cover; reduce heat to low and cook about 45 minutes, until chicken is tender. Increase heat; cook uncovered for 5 minutes.

4. Remove 4 large pieces chicken (about 1¼ lb); reserve for later use. Decrease heat; gradually stir in half-and-half and corn and cook about 3 minutes, until sauce is thickened. Season with additional salt and pepper, if desired.

Serve over egg noodles.

TIMESAVING STRATEGIES

- When reserved chicken is cool, refrigerate in resealable plastic bag to use Tuesday.

- Refrigerate reserved *mirepoix* (about 3 cups) to use Sunday and Wednesday.

- Refrigerate remaining half package of corn to use Thursday.

- Refrigerate remaining chicken broth to use Tuesday.

- Refrigerate at least ¾ cup wine to use Sunday.

- Split round bread loaf (see grocery list) horizontally. Freeze halves in resealable plastic bag to use Friday.

- Freeze walnut rolls in resealable plastic bags to use Tuesday.

Nutritional Information

PER SERVING: 505 cal, 55 g protein, 23 g fat, 14 g carbohydrate, 174 mg cholesterol, 420 mg sodium

Fish and Chips

Here's a practically mindless approach to stovetop fish cooking, with an extremely mild flavor for kids. This famous English-pub dish is usually deep fried—we've made it fast and lean. The chips take nearly an hour to cook, so start them first. For a splash of green, cook a 10-oz box of frozen peas to serve alongside. If you have leftover peas, save them to throw in Tuesday's salad.

2 T butter
¼ cup all-purpose flour
1 tsp fresh thyme or ½ tsp dried
½ tsp salt
¼ tsp black pepper
4 thin fish fillets (about 4 oz each), such as sole, flounder, or trout
1 lemon, cut into 8 wedges

1. Melt butter in deep 12-inch skillet over medium heat. Meanwhile, combine flour, thyme, salt, and pepper in large resealable plastic bag. Shake to mix. Add fillets to bag, one at a time; close bag and shake to coat.

2. Cook fillets about 4 minute per side, until golden brown. Fish should be opaque throughout and flake easily with a fork. Squeeze fresh lemon juice over servings, if desired.

Baked Chips

8 large russet potatoes (unpeeled)
½ cup reduced-sodium chicken broth
2 T olive oil
1 tsp ground cumin
1 tsp salt

1. Preheat oven to 500°F. Cut potatoes into 8 lengthwise wedges. In large bowl, toss potatoes with chicken broth, olive oil, cumin, and salt.

2. Lightly coat 2 baking sheets with vegetable cooking spray. Arrange potatoes in a single layer on prepared sheets. Bake 50 minutes, turning, until browned and crispy. Reserve ½ of potatoes for later use; serve remaining with fish and peas.

 TIMESAVING STRATEGIES

- Refrigerate reserved potatoes to use Wednesday.
- Refrigerate remaining chicken broth to use Tuesday.
- Make Sauce Bolognese (recipe follows). Refrigerate 4 cups to use Thursday.
- Refrigerate remaining sauce (about 6 cups) to use Monday.

Nutritional Information

PER SERVING OF FISH: 173 cal, 21 g protein, 7 g fat, 5 g carbohydrate, 73 mg cholesterol, 356 mg sodium

PER SERVING OF CHIPS: 280 cal, 5 g protein, 7 g fat, 51 g carbohydrate, 0 mg cholesterol, 16 mg sodium

Do-Ahead Sauce Bolognese

While the potatoes cook, make Monday's pasta sauce.

½ lb (2 small links) sweet Italian sausage, without casings
1 lb lean ground beef
1½ cup mirepoix *(reserved from Saturday)*
1 tsp salt
1 can (28 oz) whole tomatoes
1 can (15 oz) tomato sauce
¾ cup dry white wine
½ cup half-and-half

1. In large skillet over medium-high heat, crumble sausage and beef together. Cook about 5 minutes, breaking up any large clumps of meat with a wooden spoon, until meat loses red color. Add *mirepoix* and salt; cook 2 minutes, stirring. Add tomatoes, sauce, and wine; bring to a boil. Reduce heat and simmer 25 minutes, until flavors blend and meat is cooked through. Add half-and-half, simmer gently an additional 5 minutes. (Do not let sauce boil after adding half-and-half.)

2. With slotted spoon (you want a thicker mixture), remove 4 cups sauce from pot; place in plastic container to use Friday. Reserve remaining sauce (about 6 cups) to use Monday.

Spaghetti Bolognese

Serve with 1 pkg (10 oz) precleaned salad greens tossed with your favorite pre-pared salad dressing. Bake a loaf of frozen garlic bread according to package di-rections while the pasta cooks.

1 lb spaghetti or fettucine
6 cups Sauce Bolognese (reserved from Sunday)
½ cup (2 oz) grated Parmesan cheese

Cook pasta according to package directions; drain. Meanwhile, warm sauce in medium pot over medium-low heat. In large serving bowl, toss pasta with sauce. Garnish servings with cheese.

 TIMESAVING STRATEGIES

- Reserve remaining 1½ cup *mirepoix* to use Wednesday.

- Remove walnut rolls from freezer Tuesday morning; defrost in re-sealable bag at room temperature.

Nutritional Information

PER SERVING: 579 cal, 30 g protein, 20 g fat, 66 g carbohydrate, 69 mg cholesterol, 1134 mg sodium

Balsamic Chicken Caesar Salad

Our take on the ubiquitous restaurant main-dish salad. We've made the dressing low-fat—if you prefer, substitute a prepared Caesar salad dressing. Warm walnut rolls in the toaster oven.

½ cup reduced-sodium chicken broth
¼ cup nonfat plain yogurt
2 garlic cloves, minced
1 T balsamic vinegar
1 tsp anchovy paste
½ cup grated Parmesan cheese, divided
1¼ lb cooked chicken (reserved from Sunday), skin removed
3 plum tomatoes, sliced
1 small head (about 10 oz) Romaine lettuce, torn

1. In large serving bowl, whisk first 5 ingredients and ¼ cup of the cheese.

2. With your fingers, shred chicken from bone, dropping pieces into bowl as you shred. Toss well and let stand 10 minutes.

3. Add tomato slices and lettuce; toss and serve. Garnish servings with remaining ¼ cup cheese and black pepper, if desired.

Nutritional Information

PER SERVING: 321 cal, 52 g protein, 9 g fat, 6 g carbohydrate, 131 mg cholesterol, 366 mg sodium

Virginia Ham Hash

Hash is ideal weeknight fare—everyone loves it, and it uses only one pan. It's also a great way to use up leftovers. Make this a casual meal; serve directly from the skillet. Our favorite side dishes: warmed applesauce and toast.

2 T butter
1¼ lb baked potato slices (reserved from Sunday), cut into small chunks
1½ cup mirepoix (reserved from Saturday)
4 oz cooked Virginia or Black Forest ham slices, cut into chunks

2 plum tomatoes, cut into small chunks
2 tsp fresh thyme or 1 tsp dried thyme
½ tsp salt
¼ tsp black pepper
4 large eggs
½ cup shredded Monterey Jack cheese

1. Melt butter in heavy 12-inch skillet over medium heat. Add remaining ingredients, except eggs and cheese; cook 1 minute, stirring until well combined. With wide spatula, press down hash mixture; cook 10 minutes, without stirring.

2. Carefully turn hash, scraping up browned bits. Cook 3 minutes, without stirring. With back of spoon, make 4 indentations in hash. Crack 1 egg in each indentation; sprinkle with cheese. Cover skillet; cook 5 minutes, until eggs are just set. (Eggs will continue to cook on standing; do not overcook.)

Nutritional Information

PER SERVING: 241 cal, 16 g protein, 17 g fat, 7 g carbohydrate, 253 mg cholesterol, 887 mg sodium

Burritos Grande

4 cups Sauce Bolognese (reserved from Sunday)
½ pkg (10-oz size) frozen corn kernels, thawed
1 jalapeño pepper, seeded and diced
1 tsp ground cumin
1 to 2 tsp chili powder
6 large flour tortillas
1½ cups shredded Monterey Jack cheese
1 cup shredded iceberg lettuce
Nonfat plain yogurt, optional topping

1. Preheat oven to 350°F. In medium saucepan over medium-low heat, warm first 5 ingredients.

2. Wrap tortillas in foil; warm 5 minutes in oven.

3. To serve: Spoon sauce evenly down the center of each tortilla, sprinkle with cheese and lettuce; roll up. Top burritos with yogurt, if desired.

Spanish Rice Pilaf

Prepare 1 pkg Spanish rice mix according to package directions.

TIMESAVING STRATEGIES

- Start rice cooking and preheat oven to warm tortillas.

- Remove round loaf halves from freezer Friday morning; defrost in resealable plastic bag at room temperature.

Nutritional Information

PER SERVING: 667 cal, 31 g protein, 32 g fat, 64 g carbohydrate, 84 mg cholesterol, 1341 mg sodium

Muffuletta

The Muffuletta is a spicy, layered sandwich native to New Orleans. You can vary the ingredients as you wish. This makes one giant sandwich, which is then sliced and served in fat wedges. It will provide terrific leftovers for Saturday's lunch. Look for gardineria, a pepper and olive salad, in the olive section of your market. If unavailable, use drained, roasted red peppers. Serve with remaining iceberg salad tossed with your favorite prepared dressing.

1 round bread loaf, split into top half and bottom half
1 jar (12 oz) prepared gardineria (pepper and olive salad)
1 tsp fresh thyme leaves
½ lb thinly sliced Virginia or Black Forest ham
½ lb spicy salami, thinly sliced (or ¼ lb sweet and ¼ lb spicy)
½ lb provolone or fontina cheese, thinly sliced

1. Preheat oven to 400°F. Pull out and discard some of the fluffy insides from both halves of bread. Warm bread halves for 5 minutes, until slightly crusty. Drain gardineria, reserving juices in small bowl; stir in thyme. Brush juice mixture onto hollows of bread.

2. Place ½ the drained gardineria into bottom hollow of bread. Add layers of ham, salami, cheese, then remaining ½ of gardineria. Press sandwich together and wrap in plastic. Cover loaf with a plate, and place several unopened cans on plate to weigh down sandwich. Let rest 30 minutes. Slice into wedges to serve.

Nutritional Information

PER SERVING: 545 cal, 35 g protein, 32 g fat, 28 g carbohydrate, 90 mg cholesterol, 2113 mg sodium

New Family Favorites

This plan offers delicious comfort food. Start the week with a seared salmon fillet, with creamy spinach mashed potatoes. Save some of the salmon for Monday's California-style burritos. Extra potatoes are used in Thursday's curry chicken. On Sunday, there's a long-simmering brisket that's also used in succulent brisket sandwiches on Wednesday. Tuesday, you'll enjoy chicken and soup; Thursday it's curry. The week ends with an all-purpose pantry pasta meal, brightened by broccoli.

MENU

Saturday
Classic Seared Salmon Fillets
Spinach Mashed Potatoes
Green Salad with Buttermilk Dressing

Sunday
Braised Beef Brisket with Roasted Vegetables and Egg Noodles

Monday
Salmon Burritos with Yellow Rice and Black Beans

Tuesday
Chicken Breasts en Papillote
Cauliflower Bisque with Roasted Red-Pepper Cream
Crusty Peasant Bread

Wednesday
Hot Brisket Sandwiches with Caramelized Onions
Green Salad with Buttermilk Dressing
Sliced Oranges

Thursday
Chicken Curry with Potatoes and Green Beans
Herbed Pita Bread

Friday
Penne with Broccoli and Double Tomato Sauce
Great Garlic Bread

Produce
1 bunch fresh parsley
1 bunch fresh tarragon
1 bunch fresh cilantro
1 bunch fresh rosemary
1 bag (10 oz) precleaned salad greens
2 medium lemons
4 navel oranges
1 medium jalapeño pepper
1 head cauliflower or 16 oz frozen
1 head broccoli or 8 oz frozen
2 medium zucchini
½ lb green beans
2 medium parsnips
8 medium carrots
4 ½ lb boiling potatoes
5 medium yellow onions
2 medium shallots
2 heads garlic

Dairy/Freezer
1 block (4 oz) Parmesan cheese
1 container (8 oz) reduced-fat sour
  cream
1 quart low-fat milk
1 quart low-fat buttermilk
1 pkg (16 oz) frozen creamed
  spinach

Bread
4 large sandwich rolls
1 medium loaf (8 oz) Italian bread
1 small loaf crusty peasant bread

Groceries
2 cans (15-oz size) crushed tomatoes
4 cans (13¾-oz size) reduced-sodium
  chicken broth

1 can (15 oz) black beans
1 jar (7 oz) roasted red peppers
½ cup sun-dried tomatoes (not
  packed in oil)
1 pkg large pita bread
1 pkg large tortillas (You'll need 4.)
1 bag (12 oz) egg noodles
1 box (16 oz) penne or ziti pasta
Long-grain white rice

Meat/Fish
4½ lb first-cut beef brisket, excess
  fat trimmed
6 boneless, skinless chicken-breast
  halves
6 center-cut salmon fillets (about 4
  oz each), skinned

Staples
Olive oil
Cider vinegar
Curry powder
Turmeric
Ground cinnamon
Ground cumin
Bay leaves
Granulated sugar
Salt and black pepper
Aluminum foil, large resealable plas-
  tic bags, plastic wrap

Specialty Section
White wine
Mexican beer (if desired)

Desserts
Your choice!

Classic Seared Salmon Fillets

Salmon is rich in flavor and a great source of heart-healthy omega-3 fatty acids.

1 T olive oil
6 center-cut salmon fillets, 4 oz each, skinned
1 tsp salt
½ tsp black pepper

1. Warm oil in large cast-iron skillet over high heat until shimmering, but not smoking.

2. Sprinkle both sides of salmon with salt and pepper. Add 3 fillets and cook 5 minutes, shaking pan once or twice to prevent sticking. Flip; cook 2 to 3 minutes. Repeat with remaining fillets. Do not overcook; fish should be slightly translucent in the center.

3. Reserve 2 fillets for later use. (See Timesaving Strategies p. 133.) Serve remaining 4 fillets with mashed potatoes.

COOKING TIP

When cooking salmon, do not crowd the pan; cook the fillets in 2 batches. Lower heat slightly before adding the second batch—no need to add more oil.

Spinach Mashed Potatoes

Here's comfort food with a healthy twist—this may get your kids to eat spinach. To save on cleanup, use boil-in-the-bag spinach—just throw the bag in with the boiling potatoes.

1 pkg (16 oz) frozen creamed spinach
4½ lb boiling (red or white) potatoes, cut into 1½ inch cubes
½ cup low-fat milk
2 tsp salt
½ tsp black pepper
1 T chopped fresh tarragon

1. Place potatoes in large pot (no need to peel); cover with cold water. Bring to a boil over high heat and simmer 12 minutes, until tender; drain. Meanwhile, prepare spinach according to package directions.

2. Reserve 1½ lb potatoes (about 4½ cups) for later use. Return remaining potatoes to pot over medium heat. Add milk, salt, and pepper. Mash with a potato masher until smooth. Stir in spinach and tarragon.

Green Salad with Buttermilk Dressing

This tasty, low-fat dressing is used three times this week. If you prefer, substitute your favorite prepared dressing.

½ cup low-fat buttermilk
¼ cup reduced-fat sour cream
1 T chopped fresh Italian parsley
1 T fresh lemon juice
1 T grated Parmesan cheese
1 medium shallot, minced
1 small clove garlic, minced
½ tsp granulated sugar
½ tsp salt
½ tsp black pepper
½ bag (12-oz size) precleaned salad greens

1. In medium jar with tight-fitting lid, shake all ingredients except salad greens until well combined. (You should have about ¾ cup.)

2. In large serving bowl, toss ¼ cup dressing with salad greens. Serve immediately.

TIMESAVING STRATEGIES

- When reserved salmon is cool, refrigerate to use Monday.

- When reserved potatoes are cool, refrigerate to use Thursday.

- Refrigerate unused Buttermilk Dressing to use Wednesday and Friday.

- Prepare Parsley Spread (recipe follows); refrigerate to use Thursday.

- Prepare Great Garlic Bread (recipe follows); freeze to use Friday.

- Freeze rolls in resealable bag to use Wednesday.

- Cut peasant bread into thick wedges; freeze in resealable bag to use Tuesday.

Nutritional Information

PER SERVING OF SALMON: 214 cal, 23 g protein, 13 g fat, 1 g carbohydrate, 74 mg cholesterol, 589 mg sodium

PER SERVING OF POTATOES: 411 cal, 10 g protein, 6 g fat, 78 g carbohydrate, 15 mg cholesterol, 697 mg sodium.

PER SERVING OF DRESSING: 9 cal, 1 g protein, trace fat, 1 g carbohydrate, 1 mg cholesterol, 18 mg sodium

Make-Ahead Parsley Spread

Here's a simple herb oil to spread on Thursday's pita toasts.

3 T chopped fresh Italian parsley
2 T olive oil
¼ tsp salt
¼ tsp black pepper

In small jar with tight-fitting lid, shake all ingredients until blended. Refrigerate until ready to use.

Freeze-for-Friday Great Garlic Bread

Adjust the amount of garlic used according to your family's tastes.

2 T olive oil
5 cloves garlic, minced
¼ tsp salt
1 loaf (8 oz) Italian bread, split

In small bowl, combine oil, garlic, and salt. Spread evenly on cut sides of bread. Place bread halves back together; wrap in foil. Freeze to use Friday.

Braised Beef Brisket with Roasted Vegetables

Braising, or gently simmering meat in liquid until fork-tender, requires time but little effort. Ask your butcher to leave a thin layer of fat when trimming to preserve juiciness. Just before serving, cook up a pot of egg noodles for a homey side dish.

*4½ lb first-cut beef brisket, excess fat
    trimmed*
1 tsp salt
1 tsp black pepper
1 large sprig fresh rosemary
4 medium carrots, thickly sliced
*2 medium onions, cut into 6 wedges
    each*

2 medium parsnips, thickly sliced
1 T olive oil
1 T minced fresh rosemary
2 cups reduced-sodium chicken broth
1 can (15 oz) crushed tomatoes
1 cup white wine
4 large garlic cloves, crushed
4 bay leaves

1. **Preheat oven** to 500°F; place oven rack in lowest position. Rub salt and pepper into brisket, then place, fat side down, in large, deep roasting pan. Add rosemary sprig to pan; roast for 15 minutes.

2. **In medium bowl,** toss carrots, onions, and parsnips with oil and chopped rosemary. Remove pan from oven; flip roast fat side up. Add vegetables around meat in bottom of pan; roast 30 minutes. Meanwhile, in medium bowl, combine broth, tomatoes, wine, garlic, and bay leaves.

3. **Reduce** temperature to 275°F. Remove pan from oven; pour tomato mixture over brisket and vegetables. Tightly cover pan (with lid or foil); roast 3 hours. Meat is done when a double-pronged fork can be inserted without resistance.

4. **Remove vegetables** to platter; cover with foil to keep warm. Place brisket on cutting board; tent with foil and let stand 10 minutes. Pour pan juices into a strainer set over a bowl; press down on solids with spoon to extract all juices.

Discard solids. You should have about 2 cups braising sauce. Reserve 1 cup for later use. Let remaining sauce stand until fat rises to the top; skim off with a spoon.

5. Cut brisket in half; reserve half for later use. Thinly slice remaining piece against the grain. Serve with roasted vegetables, egg noodles, and skimmed sauce.

 TIMESAVING STRATEGIES

- When reserved beef is cool, refrigerate to use Wednesday.

- Refrigerate reserved braising sauce to use Wednesday.

- While beef cooks, prepare Cauliflower Bisque (recipe follows); refrigerate to use Tuesday.

- Prepare Roasted Red-Pepper Cream (recipe follows); refrigerate to use Tuesday.

- Prepare Shredded Vegetables (recipe follows); refrigerate to use Tuesday.

Nutritional Information

PER SERVING BRISKET AND VEGETABLES: 417 cal, 38 g protein, 19 g fat, 16 g carbohydrate, 120 mg cholesterol, 595 mg sodium

Cook-Ahead Trio

Cauliflower Bisque

Puree this soup in batches—never fill the blender more than ⅔ full with a hot liquid. Always begin blending at low speed, gradually increasing to high.

Florets from 1 large head cauliflower or 2 bags (8-oz size) cauliflower florets
1 T olive oil
1 medium onion, coarsely chopped
3 cups reduced-sodium chicken broth
2 cups low-fat buttermilk

1. Coarsely chop florets. Warm oil in large saucepan or soup pot over medium-high heat. Add onion; cook 3 minutes, or until softened, stirring often. Add cauliflower; cook 5 minutes, stirring. Add broth and buttermilk. Bring to a simmer; let simmer, partially covered, 30 minutes, until cauliflower is tender. The soup will look curdled.

2. In blender or food processor, puree soup, working in batches. Transfer to plastic container; refrigerate for later use.

Roasted Red-Pepper Cream

This versatile blend can be used as a dip, a sandwich spread, or a colorful addition to a soup or pasta sauce.

1 jar (7 oz) roasted red peppers, drained
¼ cup reduced-fat sour cream

In blender or food processor, combine ingredients; process until smoothly pureed. Refrigerate for later use.

YIELD: ABOUT ¾ CUP

Shredded Vegetables

As long as you've got the food processor out, save yourself some chopping. If you haven't got a food processor, slice veggies into matchstick-size pieces.

4 medium carrots, halved lengthwise
2 medium zucchini, halved lengthwise

In food processor fitted with shredding disk, shred carrots and zucchini (no need to peel). Store in plastic container, covered with water. Refrigerate to use Tuesday.

Salmon Burritos with Yellow Rice and Black Beans

COOKING TIP

Turmeric isn't essential here—it mainly adds a golden color.

For a change of pace, we've added salmon to the traditional rice and bean burrito. Of course you can leave it out if it doesn't please your picky eaters.

2 tsp olive oil
½ medium onion, chopped
1 tsp ground cumin
½ tsp turmeric
1 cup long-grain white rice
1 tsp salt
1 can (15 oz) black beans, drained and rinsed

1 medium jalapeño pepper, seeded and minced
½ cup coarsely chopped fresh cilantro
¼ cup fresh lime juice (from 2 limes)
2 salmon fillets (reserved from Saturday)
4 large (10-inch size) flour tortillas
½ cup reduced-fat sour cream

1. Preheat oven to 200°F. Warm 1 tsp of the oil in medium saucepan over medium heat. Add onion, cumin, and turmeric; cook 2 minutes, stirring. Add rice and cook 1 minute more, stirring. Add salt and 2 cups water; increase heat and bring to a boil. Reduce heat to low; cover and simmer 18 minutes.

2. Stir in beans, pepper, ¼ cup of the cilantro, and 2 T of the lime juice. Cover and let stand 5 minutes.

3. Meanwhile, wrap tortillas in foil and place in preheated oven for 5 minutes, until warm.

4. Using your fingers or a fork, flake salmon into bite-size pieces. Warm remaining 1 tsp oil in medium skillet over medium heat. Add salmon and remaining 2 T lime juice; cook 3 minutes until heated through. Gently stir in remaining ¼ cup cilantro.

5. To serve, fill each burrito with rice and beans, then top with salmon. Garnish with sour cream. Serve any remaining rice and beans on the side.

TIMESAVING STRATEGY

- Remove peasant-bread wedges from freezer Tuesday morning; defrost, in resealable bag, at room temperature.

Nutritional Information

PER SERVING: 652 cal, 31 g protein, 17 g fat, 92 g carbohydrate, 56 mg cholesterol, 598 mg sodium

Chicken Breasts en Papillote

E*n papillote* is the French term for cooking something wrapped in parchment paper or foil to seal in aroma and flavor. It's a terrific low-fat technique.

6 boneless, skinless chicken-breast halves
1 T plus 2 tsp olive oil
2½ tsp salt
1½ tsp black pepper
Shredded carrots and zucchini (reserved from Sunday), drained
3 T chopped fresh parsley
1 medium lemon, thinly sliced
½ cup white wine

1. Preheat oven to 350°F. Tear off four 12-inch squares of foil. Stack, then fold squares in half. Cut to make a heart shape. Unfold and spread four foil hearts out on counter; drizzle ½ tsp of the oil in center of each heart. Place 1 breast on each foil heart on top of oil; sprinkle with 1 tsp of the salt and ½ tsp of the pepper. Set aside 2 remaining breasts.

2. In medium bowl, toss carrot and zucchini with 1 tsp of the salt and ½ tsp of the pepper. Top each of the 4 breasts with equal amounts of vegetables, chopped parsley, lemon slices, and wine. Bring up heart edges and crimp edges to seal tightly. Place on baking sheet and bake 30 minutes.

3. Meanwhile, cut the 2 remaining breasts into 1-inch cubes; place in 9-inch square pan. Toss with remaining 1 T oil, ½ tsp salt, and ½ tsp pepper. Bake in oven with foil packages 6 minutes, or until chicken is cooked through. Reserve for later use.

4. Serve chicken and vegetables immediately. If desired, serve directly out of foil packages.

Cauliflower Bisque with Roasted Red-Pepper Cream

This elegant soup is low in calories and fat. There is enough to serve four for dinner, plus extra for a workday lunch.

Cauliflower Bisque (assembled on Sunday)
1 tsp salt
½ tsp black pepper
2 T chopped fresh tarragon
½ cup Roasted Red-Pepper Cream (reserved from Sunday)

In medium saucepan over medium heat, add salt and pepper to soup and warm 10 minutes, until heated through. Stir in tarragon. Ladle into soup bowls; swirl 2 T pepper cream into each.

 TIMESAVING STRATEGIES

- Since the oven is on you can prepare chicken for Thursday night's curry while making the chicken en papillote.

- Wrap wedges of peasant bread in foil and warm for dinner tonight.

- When reserved chicken is cool, wrap well and refrigerate to use Thursday.

- Remove rolls from freezer Wednesday morning for Wednesday's dinner; defrost in resealable bag at room temperature.

Nutritional Information

PER SERVING OF CHICKEN: 299 cal, 45 g protein, 8 g fat, 6 g carbohydrate, 120 mg cholesterol, 389 mg sodium
PER SERVING OF BISQUE: 120 cal, 7 g protein, 5 g fat, 14 g carbohydrate, 5 mg cholesterol, 600 mg sodium

Wednesday's Dinner: Hot Brisket Sandwiches with Caramelized Onions; Green Salad with Buttermilk Dressing; Sliced Oranges

— SERVES 4 —

Hot Brisket Sandwiches with Caramelized Onions

Slow-cooking onions with a little sugar makes them a great topping for sandwiches, pizzas, and pastas. To round out the meal, toss a salad using remaining lettuce and cup ¼ buttermilk dressing.

1 tsp olive oil
1½ medium onions, thinly sliced
1 tsp salt
1 T cider vinegar
1 tsp granulated sugar
Beef brisket (reserved from Sunday), thinly sliced
1 cup braising sauce (reserved from Sunday)
4 sandwich rolls

1. Preheat oven to 350°F. Warm oil in large skillet over medium heat. Add onions and salt; cook 10 minutes, stirring often. Stir in vinegar and sugar; cook 15 minutes more, until softened and light golden brown, stirring often.

2. Meanwhile, spread meat slices in 9-inch square baking pan. Remove and discard hardened fat from the top of the braising sauce. Spoon liquid over meat. Cover pan with foil; warm in preheated oven 25 minutes. Wrap rolls in foil; warm in oven alongside meat.

3. To serve: Sandwich meat and onions between sliced roll halves.

Nutritional Information

PER SERVING: 533 cal, 50 g protein, 26 g fat, 21 g carbohydrate, 136 mg cholesterol, 927 mg sodium

Chicken Curry with Potatoes and Green Beans

1 T olive oil
2 garlic cloves, minced
1 medium shallot, minced
1 T curry powder
Roasted chicken cubes (reserved from Tuesday)
2 cups reduced-sodium chicken broth
1½ lb potatoes (reserved from Sunday), cut into ½-inch cubes
½ lb green beans, cut into 1-inch pieces
¼ tsp cinnamon
⅓ cup chopped fresh cilantro

1. Warm oil in large skillet over medium heat. Add garlic and shallots; cook 1 minute, stirring.

2. Add curry; stir to absorb oil.

3. Add chicken; stir to coat. Add broth, potatoes, beans, and cinnamon. Simmer 10 to 12 minutes, until sauce is thickened and beans are done, stirring occasionally. Stir in cilantro.

Herbed Pita Bread

Preheat oven to 350°F. Lightly spread the tops of 4 pita breads with Parsley Spread (reserved from Saturday). Place on baking sheet; bake 10 minutes, until warm. Cut into quarters.

TIMESAVING STRATEGY

- Remove garlic bread from freezer Friday morning for dinner that night; defrost, in foil at room temperature.

Nutritional Information

PER SERVING OF CHICKEN CURRY: 322 cal, 27 g protein, 6 g fat, 40 g carbohydrate, 60 mg cholesterol, 79 mg sodium

PER SERVING OF PITA: 226 cal, 6 g protein, 7 g fat, 34 g carbohydrate, 0 mg cholesterol, 457 mg sodium

Penne with Broccoli and Double Tomato Sauce

Celebrate Friday with a family favorite: Pasta with tomato sauce and homemade garlic bread. Got leftover parsley or grated Parmesan cheese? Toss either or both into the pasta at the end.

½ cup sun-dried tomatoes (not packed in oil), thinly sliced
1 T olive oil
2 cloves garlic, minced
1 can (15 oz) crushed tomatoes
2 tsp chopped fresh rosemary
1 tsp salt
½ tsp granulated sugar
¼ tsp black pepper
¼ cup Roasted Red-Pepper Cream (reserved from Sunday)
1 lb penne pasta
Florets from 2 large broccoli stalks, or 1 bag (8 oz) broccoli florets
¼ cup grated Parmesan cheese, optional

1. In small bowl, combine sun-dried tomatoes and 1 cup hot water. Soak for 15 minutes. Drain, reserving soaking liquid.

2. Warm oil in large nonstick skillet over medium-high heat. Add garlic and drained sun-dried tomatoes. Cook 1 minute, stirring. Add reserved soaking liquid; bring to a boil. Boil 5 minutes, until sauce is reduced.

3. Stir in tomatoes, rosemary, salt, sugar, and black pepper. Reduce heat; simmer 10 minutes, until slightly thickened.

4. Stir in pepper cream to warm through.

5. Meanwhile, prepare pasta according to package directions. Add broccoli during last 4 minutes of cooking.

6. Drain; return pasta and broccoli to pot. Add sauce; toss to coat. Garnish servings with cheese, if desired.

Great Garlic Bread

1. Preheat oven to 400°F. Take bread out of freezer (it was prepared and frozen on Saturday) and put directly into oven.

2. Bake foil-wrapped loaf 10 minutes, until warmed through. Slice and serve immediately.

Nutritional Information

PER SERVING OF PASTA: 256 cal, 9 g protein, 5 g fat, 45 g carbohydrate, 1 mg cholesterol, 868 mg sodium

PER SERVING OF BREAD: 219 cal, 5 g protein, 9 g fat, 30 g carbohydrate, 0 mg cholesterol, 465 mg sodium

Hale and Hearty

Saturday's dinner stars a roast surrounded by roasted tomatoes and root vegetables. The tender beef is tossed in a salad on Monday, and makes a classic Beef Burgundy to freeze for a future night. The savory tomatoes become a homemade tomato sauce for Tuesday's lasagna. Roasted vegetables find a second home in the tomato sauce, the Beef Burgundy, and Sunday's lamb and potato dish. Thursday night is a pantry meal of couscous and tuna that's ready in 10 minutes.

MENU

Saturday
Roasted Rib-eye with Root Vegetables
Oven-Roasted Tomatoes
French Bread

Sunday
Garlic Lamb Chops on a Potato Bed
Lemony Green Beans

Monday
Bistro Steak and Pear Salad
French Toasts

Tuesday
Spinach Lasagna
Green Salad

Wednesday
California Chicken Salad
Dinner Rolls

Thursday
Mediterranean Couscous and Tuna
Warmed Pita Rounds

Friday
Quick Beef Burgundy
Egg Noodles

GROCERY LIST FOR THE WEEK

Produce

1 large lemon
1 large ripe pear
½ lb seedless green or red grapes
1 bag (10 oz) fresh spinach leaves
1 bag (16 oz) precleaned salad greens
1 Belgian endive
1 bunch fresh Italian parsley
1 bunch fresh tarragon
1 lb green beans
1 pkg (10 oz) button mushrooms
4 lb plum tomatoes (about 30)
1 pkg (16 oz) baby carrots
4 lb Yukon gold or other all-purpose potato
1 head garlic
1 large shallot
1 small red onion
4 medium yellow onions

Packaged

1 can (13¾-oz size) reduced-sodium beef broth
1 box (8 oz) oven-ready lasagna noodles
1 cup sliced almonds
1 bottle (8 oz) prepared Italian salad dressing
2 cans (13¾-oz size) reduced-sodium chicken broth
1 box (6–8 oz) seasoned grain or couscous mix
1 large can or 2 small cans (6 oz) water-packed albacore tuna
1 can (15 oz) chick peas

Dairy

4 oz Parmesan cheese (or 1 cup grated)
1 container (15 oz) part-skim ricotta cheese
Eggs (You'll need 2.)
1 bag (8 oz) shredded mozzarella cheese
1 container (8 oz) reduced-fat sour cream

Meat

4 lb well-trimmed boneless beef rib-eye roast, small end
2 lb lamb shoulder chops (3 or 4 chops)
3 lb boneless, skinless chicken-breast halves

Bread

2 French baguettes (about 12 inches in length)
4 large dinner rolls

Staples

Olive oil
Reduced-fat mayonnaise
Dried thyme
White-wine vinegar
Dried oregano
Cornstarch
Salt and black pepper
Aluminum foil, resealable plastic bags, plastic wrap

Roasted Rib-eye with Root Vegetables

Start the week with a tender roasted beef, served with a bounty of root vegetables and tomatoes.

4 lb well-trimmed boneless beef rib-eye roast, small end
4 large cloves garlic, minced
2 tsp dried thyme leaves
1 tsp black pepper
3 T olive oil
1 tsp salt
4 lb medium Yukon gold or other all-purpose potato, halved
1 pkg (16 oz) baby carrots
4 medium onions, cut into 8 thick wedges each

1. Preheat oven to 350°F. Place roast, fat side up, on rack in large, shallow roasting pan. In small bowl, combine garlic, thyme, and pepper; press ½ of mixture evenly into surface of roast. To seasoning mixture remaining in bowl, add oil and salt; set aside.

2. In large bowl, toss potatoes, carrots, onion wedges, and remaining seasoning mixture; add to bottom of roasting pan. Roast, uncovered, about 2 hours. Meat is done when meat thermometer registers 135°F.

3. Remove roast to carving board; let rest 15 minutes. Warm a baguette in the oven while the beef rests.

4. Slice roast into 3 equal pieces (about 1 lb each). Reserve 2 pieces beef for later use.

5. With tongs or a slotted spoon, pick out 1½ cups of the roasted onions; reserve for later use. Reserve ½ of the potatoes for later use (about 3 cups). Slice remaining piece of beef; serve with remaining roasted vegetables.

Oven-Roasted Tomatoes

Here's a solution for the scarcity of fresh tomatoes during the winter. Coat little plum tomatoes (available year-round) with olive oil and roast until soft and juicy.

4 lb plum tomatoes (about 30), halved lengthwise and cored
¼ cup olive oil
1 T salt
½ tsp black pepper

1. In large roasting pan, toss all ingredients. Roast, alongside beef, for 1 hour, until soft and shriveled.

2. Serve 8 halves; reserve remaining tomatoes and any pan juices for tomato sauce (see recipe below).

 TIMESAVING STRATEGIES

- Let 2 reserved pieces of beef cool. Wrap well and refrigerate 1 piece to use Monday. Use the other reserved piece to make Quick Beef Burgundy (see recipe below); freeze to use on Friday night.

- Reserve 1½ cups roasted onions to make Oven-Roasted Tomato Sauce and Quick Beef Burgundy (see recipes below).

- Reserve remaining roasted tomatoes and any pan juices and make Oven-Roasted Tomato Sauce (see recipe below); refrigerate to use Tuesday.

- Refrigerate reserved roasted potatoes (about 3 cups) to use Sunday.

- Reserve ¾ cup of the red wine to make Quick Beef Burgundy.

- Freeze remaining baguette in resealable plastic bag to use Monday.

- Freeze dinner rolls in resealable plastic bag to use Wednesday.

PER SERVING BEEF: 296 cal, 30 g protein, 19 g fat, 0 g carbohydrate, 88 mg cholesterol, 79 mg sodium

PER SERVING TOMATOES: 307 cal, 6 g protein, 2 g fat, 68 g carbohydrate, 0 mg cholesterol, 306 mg sodium

Make-Ahead Oven-Roasted Tomato Sauce

Oven-roasted tomatoes (reserved from above)
1 cup roasted onions (reserved from above)
1 T fresh oregano or 1 tsp dried

1. In blender, puree all ingredients. (Puree in batches, if necessary.) Taste and adjust salt and pepper as needed.

2. Pour into plastic container; refrigerate to use Tuesday.

YIELD: ABOUT 3 CUPS

Quick Beef Burgundy

If you can bear it, go back into the kitchen after dinner and throw together this speedy version of the French classic. If you can't bear it, refrigerate the beef and do it on Sunday.

1 T olive oil
1 pkg (10 oz) mushrooms, thinly sliced
¾ cup dry red wine (Burgundy or Zinfandel)
½ tsp dried thyme
½ cup reduced-sodium beef broth
1 T cornstarch
1 lb roast beef (reserved from above), thinly sliced
½ cup roasted onions (reserved from above)

1. Warm oil in medium-heavy saucepan over medium heat. Add mushrooms; cook 2 minutes, gently stirring. Stir in wine and thyme.

2. In small bowl, combine broth, cornstarch, and ¼ cup water. Slowly pour mixture into the mushroom wine sauce in the skillet, still over medium heat. Bring to a simmer; let simmer 6 minutes. Add beef slices and onions; stir to blend flavors. Let cool; pour into plastic container and freeze to use on Friday.

Garlic Lamb Chops on a Potato Bed

If your kids like crispy potatoes, this is the dish for them. Try to slice the potatoes about ⅛-inch thick—thicker slices will take longer to cook.

3 cups roasted potatoes (reserved from Saturday)
2 lb lamb-shoulder chops (3 to 4 chops)
1 tsp salt, divided
½ tsp black pepper, divided
1 T olive oil
4 cloves garlic, thinly sliced
1 cup reduced-sodium beef broth
¼ cup grated Parmesan cheese

1. Preheat oven to 400°F. Slice potatoes thinly; spread evenly in 9- by 13-inch baking dish. Sprinkle with ½ tsp of the salt and ¼ tsp of the pepper. Bake 15 minutes, until warmed and slightly browned. Remove pan from oven; turn on broiler.

2. Sprinkle lamb on both sides with remaining salt and pepper. Warm oil in large nonstick skillet over medium-high heat until hot. Add lamb; brown about 2 minutes per side. Add garlic slices and broth to skillet; cover and simmer 5 minutes.

3. Arrange lamb on top of potatoes; sprinkle potatoes with cheese. (Discard lamb cooking liquid.) Broil 4 minutes, until lamb is cooked through. If potatoes start to burn, move pan farther away from heat source.

Lemony Green Beans

Bright green beans are tossed with olive oil and lemon in this simple side dish. For a lowfat option, reduce oil to 1 tsp.

1 lb green beans, trimmed
1 large lemon
1 T olive oil
½ small red onion, very thinly sliced
¼ tsp salt

1. In medium saucepan, cover beans with water. Bring to a boil; reduce heat to medium and cook, uncovered, about 4 minutes, until tender-crisp. Drain and set aside.

2. Meanwhile, from lemon, squeeze 2 T juice. (Reserve 1 T for later use.) In same pan over medium heat, combine lemon juice with remaining ingredients; cook about 2 minutes, stirring. Return beans to pot; cook 1 minute, stirring to blend flavors. Reserve 1 cup beans for later use. Serve remaining beans hot.

 TIMESAVING STRATEGIES

- Refrigerate reserved 1 cup green beans to use Monday.

- Refrigerate reserved 1 T fresh lemon juice to use Thursday.

- Refrigerate remaining ½ red onion to use Thursday.

- Assemble lasagna (see recipe below); cover and refrigerate to use Tuesday.

- Remove French bread from freezer Monday morning; defrost in resealable bag at room temperature.

Nutritional Information

PER SERVING LAMB AND POTATOES: 517 cal, 48 g protein, 25 g fat, 24 g carbohydrate, 153 mg cholesterol, 883 mg sodium
PER SERVING GREEN BEANS: 52 cal, 2 g protein, 3 g fat, 6 g carbohydrate, 0 mg cholesterol, 112 mg sodium

Do-Ahead Spinach Lasagna

Let's face it—lasagna is a time-consuming dish to make. Our solution: Assemble in advance, so it's ready to pop in the oven Tuesday night.

1 pkg (8 oz) oven-ready lasagna noodles
½ bag (10 oz) fresh spinach, trimmed and finely chopped
1 container (15 oz) part-skim ricotta cheese
2 large eggs
½ cup grated Parmesan cheese
Oven-roasted tomato sauce (reserved from Saturday)
1 bag (8 oz) shredded mozzarella cheese

1. In large bowl or sink filled with hot water, soak noodles while you prepare filling. In large bowl, combine spinach, ricotta, eggs, and Parmesan; set aside.

2. Pour a thin layer of tomato sauce on bottom of 9- by 13-inch pan. Tilt pan to assure sauce covers entire surface. Place 1 layer of lasagna noodles on top of sauce. (No need to dry noodles). Cover noodles with another thin layer of sauce, then spoon ½ of the ricotta mixture over sauce. Top with ½ cup mozzarella, then layer noodles, sauce, the remaining ricotta, ½ cup mozzarella, and final layer of noodles. Top with the remaining sauce and mozzarella. Cover with plastic wrap, then foil. Refrigerate to use Tuesday.

Bistro Steak and Pear Salad

We've combined spinach and lettuce in this salad, but you can use any green. Set aside some beef and beans to serve plain if your kids don't care for salad.

1 lb roast beef (reserved from Saturday), cut into thin strips
1 cup lemony green beans (reserved from Sunday), halved
½ pkg (10 oz) fresh spinach, washed and trimmed
¼ pkg (16-oz size) precleaned salad greens
1 firm, ripe pear, cut into wedges
½ cup sliced almonds
¼ cup prepared Italian salad dressing
2 T chopped fresh tarragon

In large bowl gently toss all ingredients. Serve immediately. Reserving remaining almonds for Thursday.

French Toasts

Preheat broiler. Cut 1 French baguette into thick diagonal slices. Sprinkle 1 side of each slice with ¼ cup Parmesan cheese. Broil until cheese melts.

Nutritional Information

PER SERVING SALAD: 520 cal, 36 g protein, 36 g fat, 15 g carbohydrate, 88 mg cholesterol, 253 mg sodium
PER SERVING TOASTS: 184 cal, 8 g protein, 4 g fat, 30 g carbohydrate, 5 mg cholesterol, 461 mg sodium

Spinach Lasagna

This dish was assembled on Sunday.

1. If possible take lasagna out of the fridge a couple of hours before baking.

2. Preheat oven to 350°F. Remove foil and plastic wrap from lasagna; bring to room temperature. Recover with foil; bake 35 minutes.

3. Remove foil; bake 10 to 15 minutes longer, until cheese melts and sauce bubbles. Let sit 10 minutes before serving.

4. Serve with green salad—toss remaining salad greens with prepared salad dressing and ½ can chickpeas, drained and rinsed.

Nutritional Information

PER SERVING: 393 cal, 28 g protein, 21 g fat, 24 g carbohydrate, 119 mg cholesterol, 1008 mg sodium

Do-Ahead Poached Chicken Breasts

Since you don't have to cook tonight, you can get a jump on Wednesday's dinner.

3 lb boneless, skinless chicken-breast halves
½ tsp salt
2 cans (13¾-oz size) reduced-sodium chicken broth

1. Arrange chicken in single layer in 9- by 13-inch baking pan; sprinkle with salt. Pour broth to just cover chicken.

2. Cover pan with foil; bake along with lasagna about 30 minutes, until cooked through.

3. Allow chicken to cool in liquid; discard liquid. When chicken is cool, re-frigerate in resealable bag to use Wednesday.

GAME PLAN

This salad is so tasty we've made the recipe to serve 6, so you have leftovers to bring to work for lunch. Use whatever seedless grapes are in season. Serve with rolls warmed in toaster oven or broiler.

California Chicken Salad

½ cup reduced-fat mayonnaise
½ cup reduced-fat sour cream
1 T white-wine or tarragon vinegar
2½–3 lb poached chicken breasts (reserved from Tuesday)
1 large Belgian endive or celery stalk, thickly sliced
1 medium shallot, sliced
1½ cups (about ½ lb) seedless green or red grapes
½ cup sliced almonds
2 T fresh tarragon, chopped, or 1 T dried

1. In large serving bowl, combine first 3 ingredients.

2. Dice chicken into ¾-inch chunks; add to bowl.

3. Add remaining ingredients; toss to coat. Serve over salad greens.

Nutritional Information

PER SERVING: 412 cal, 55 g protein, 15 g fat, 14 g carbohydrate, 148 mg cholesterol, 369 mg sodium

Mediterranean Couscous and Tuna

This is one of those dishes that features pantry staples—perfect for those nights when there's nary a fresh ingredient in the house.

1 box (6 oz) seasoned couscous or grain mix
1 large can (12 oz) or 2 cans (6 oz) water-packed white albacore tuna
½ small red onion, thinly sliced (reserved from Sunday)
¼ cup prepared Italian salad dressing
1 T fresh lemon juice (reserved from Sunday)
½ tsp salt
½ can (15 oz-size) chickpeas, drained and rinsed
2 T fresh parsley, chopped
8 pita rounds

Prepare couscous according to package directions. In large bowl, combine remaining ingredients. Stir in couscous. Serve warm or at room temperature with warmed pita rounds.

TIMESAVING STRATEGY

- Remove Quick Beef Burgundy from freezer; defrost overnight in refrigerator for Friday's dinner. Never defrost meat at room temperature.

Nutritional Information

PER SERVING: 310 cal, 27 g protein, 9 g fat, 45 g carbohydrate, 21 mg cholesterol, 630 mg sodium

Quick Beef Burgundy

8 oz wide egg noodles
Beef burgundy (assembled and frozen on Sunday), thawed
¼ cup chopped fresh parsley, if desired

1. Prepare noodles according to package directions; drain.

2. Meanwhile, in large saucepan over medium-low heat, warm beef dish until heated through.

3. Serve over noodles; top with parsley, if desired.

Nutritional Information

PER SERVING: 424 cal, 37 g protein, 23 g fat, 18 g carbohydrate, 107 mg cholesterol, 94 mg sodium

A Touch of the Tropics

Grilled shrimp accompanied by a mango-lime salsa gives a festive island start to the week. We're making you work on Saturday, preparing exotic sauces that are the flavor punch behind meals for Saturday, Wednesday, and Friday.

On Sunday, enjoy grilled steak and cook up some chicken and vegetables, too. The chicken shows up on Monday and Wednesday. Leftover steak makes a Tuesday night sandwich. On Thursday, the vegetables get wrapped up in tortillas with rice and cheese. The Asian flavors of peanut, sesame, and lime combine in Friday's pasta dish.

MENU

Saturday
Shrimp Fajitas with Mango-Lime Salsa
Spicy Black Beans and Rice

Sunday
Grilled Steak au Poivre
Warm New-Potato and Asparagus Salad
Corn on the Cob

Monday
Blue-Ribbon Chicken Salad

Tuesday
Beefeaters' Steak Sandwiches
Balsamic Green and Yellow Beans

Wednesday
Chicken Pad Thai
Fresh Plums

Thursday
Grilled-Vegetable Wraps
Tossed Green Salad

Friday
Peanut-Sesame Noodles
Cool Cucumber Salad

Produce
6 large limes
2 large lemons
2 ripe mangoes
1 pint fresh strawberries
1 bunch watercress
1 bag (16 oz) precleaned salad greens
2 bunches fresh cilantro
1 bunch fresh Italian parsley
1 bunch fresh dill
1 large bunch scallions
4 large cucumbers
1 ripe avocado (optional)
3 large red bell peppers
1 jalapeño pepper
2 medium tomatoes
6 ears fresh corn
½ lb green beans
½ lb yellow beans
½ lb snow peas
½ lb asparagus
1 cup (4 oz) mung-bean sprouts
1 lb small new potatoes
3 medium red onions
1 head garlic

Canned/Packaged
1 jar smooth peanut butter
1 jar black peppercorns (¼ cup)
1 jar (8 oz) prepared balsamic salad
   dressing
1 jar Thai fish sauce
1 can (16 oz) black beans
1 pkg (12–16 oz) vermicelli or linguine
1 pkg (8 oz) rice stick noodles
1 pkg (3½ oz) boil-in-bag long-
   grain rice
½ cup (2 oz) pecans or walnuts

Meat/Fish
8 boneless, skinless chicken-breast
   halves (about 2½ lb)
32 large shrimp, shelled and deveined (about 1¼ lb)
3 T-Bone steaks, 1 inch thick

Dairy
8 oz reduced-fat sour cream
4 oz blue cheese
4 oz Jarlsberg or Swiss cheese

Bread/Starches
4 large sandwich or French rolls
1 loaf pumpernickel (8 slices)
Large flour tortillas (12)

Staples
Olive oil
Rice-wine vinegar
Asian sesame oil
Reduced-fat mayonnaise
Reduced-sodium soy sauce
Red-pepper flakes
Prepared horseradish
Ground cumin
Granulated sugar
Salt and black pepper
Aluminum foil, plastic wrap, and
   large resealable plastic bags
Wooden skewers (10 inches; You'll
   need 6.)

Desserts
Your choice!

Saturday after shopping, is prep time. First you'll make the special sauces, then get a jump on the rest of the week.

Lime-Cilantro Sauce

From 2 limes, grate 2 tsp peel; from 6 limes, squeeze ¾ cup juice. Refrigerate separately to use Saturday and Wednesday. To make Lime-Cilantro Sauce for Saturday and Wednesday:

3 cloves garlic, halved
1 cup packed fresh cilantro leaves
2 tsp grated lime peel
½ cup fresh lime juice
½ cup olive oil
1 tsp salt
½ tsp black pepper

In food processor fitted with metal blade, drop garlic through feed tube with motor running. Add remaining ingredients; process until blended. Transfer to plastic container; refrigerate until ready to use.

Peanut-Sesame Sauce

This is for use Wednesday and Friday.

1 clove garlic, halved
½ cup smooth peanut butter
2 T reduced-sodium soy sauce
1 T rice-wine vinegar
1 T Asian sesame oil
¼ tsp red-pepper flakes

In food processor fitted with metal blade, drop garlic through feed tube with motor running. Add remaining ingredients and ½ cup hot water. Process to blend, adding additional hot water if necessary to create a thick but pourable sauce. Transfer to plastic container; refrigerate until ready to use.

Lemon Marinade

From 2 lemons, grate 1 T peel and squeeze 6 T juice. Refrigerate separately to use Saturday. To make marinade:

¼ cup olive oil
1 T lemon peel
¼ cup fresh lemon juice
1 tsp salt
½ tsp black pepper

In jar with tight-fitting lid, shake all ingredients until blended.

TIMESAVING STRATEGIES

- Rinse 8 boneless, skinless chicken-breast halves; pat dry with paper towels. In large resealable plastic bag, combine chicken with 6 T of the Lemon Marinade. In another large resealable plastic bag, combine 2 red onions, thickly sliced, with remaining 2 T of the marinade. Refrigerate to use Sunday.

- Freeze sandwich rolls (see grocery list) in resealable plastic bags to use Monday.

Shrimp Fajitas with Mango-Lime Salsa

Part of the fun of serving fajitas is the do-it-yourself assembly of this Southwestern favorite. The colorful salsa can be spooned into the fajitas, used as a dip for chips, or eaten with a fork.

32 large shrimp (about 1¼ lb)
½ cup plus 2 T (10 T) Lime-Cilantro Sauce
2 ripe mangoes, peeled and diced, or 3 cups diced pineapple
1 red pepper, diced
1 jalapeño pepper, seeded and diced

1 ripe avocado, peeled and diced (optional)
½ red onion, diced
2 T fresh cilantro leaves
8 large flour tortillas
½ cup (4 oz) reduced-fat sour cream

A ripe mango will yield to gentle pressure and have a sweet fragrance. To remove the flesh from the seed, halve the fruit vertically, sliding the knife along the seed. Repeat on the other side, so you have two large pieces. Then peel the halves.

1. Soak 6 thick wooden skewers (each about 10 inches long) in water at least 30 minutes to prevent burning. (Wooden skewers are preferable to metal because they don't become too hot to handle when grilling.)

2. In large resealable plastic bag, combine shrimp and ½ cup (8 T) of the Lime-Cilantro Sauce; turn to coat. Refrigerate for up to 4 hours.

3. To make salsa: In medium serving bowl combine mango, red and jalapeño peppers, avocado, onion, cilantro, and the remaining 2 T Lime-Cilantro Sauce.

4. Prepare grill (high heat). Thread shrimp onto skewers. Discard marinade. Grill about 3 minutes, until bright red, turning once. The insides should be an opaque white. If desired, wrap tortillas in foil and warm on grill just before serving. Serve shrimp with salsa, tortillas, and sour cream to make fajitas.

Spicy Black Beans and Rice

We've used boil-in-bag rice here for convenience, but feel free to substitute any type of rice.

1 pkg (about 3½ oz) boil-in-bag long-grain rice
1 can (15 oz) black beans, rinsed and drained
1 T fresh lemon juice (reserved from Saturday)
1 T olive oil
1 tsp ground cumin
1 scallion, thinly sliced

Prepare rice according to package directions. In medium saucepan over medium-low heat, combine remaining ingredients and cook about 5 minutes, until warm, stirring occasionally. Serve beans over rice.

 TIMESAVING STRATEGIES

- Refrigerate remaining Lime-Cilantro Sauce to use Wednesday and Friday.

- Refrigerate remaining lime juice to use Wednesday.

- Refrigerate remaining ½ red onion to use Friday

Nutritional Information

PER SERVING OF SHRIMP AND SALSA: 609 cal, 23 g protein, 20 g fat, 86 g carbohydrate, 95 mg cholesterol, 778 mg sodium
PER SERVING OF BEANS AND RICE: 246 cal, 10 g protein, 4 g fat, 42 g carbohydrate, 0 mg cholesterol, 3 mg sodium

Grilled Steak au Poivre

The beauty of this steak dish lies in its simplicity. To crush peppercorns, smash them with the bottom of a heavy saucepan. Of course, you can substitute ground pepper, or omit the pepper entirely for the kids.

3 T-bone or porterhouse steaks, cut 1 inch thick (about 3 lb)
1 tsp salt
¼ cup coarsely crushed black peppercorns

1. Prepare grill to high heat. Sprinkle both sides of steaks with salt; coat with crushed pepper. Grill, uncovered, about 7 minutes per side for medium.

2. Transfer to cutting board; let stand 5 minutes.

3. Thinly slice 2 of the steaks; serve with potato salad and corn. Reserve third steak for later use.

Warm New-Potato and Asparagus Salad

Boiling potatoes with the skin on retains more of the vitamins and minerals. For added color and fiber, we prefer to keep the potatoes unpeeled in the salad.

1 lb small new potatoes, unpeeled
½ lb asparagus, trimmed and cut into 1-inch lengths
3 T olive oil
2 T rice-wine vinegar
½ tsp salt
¼ tsp black pepper
2 scallions, thinly sliced
3 T chopped fresh Italian parsley
¼ cup (2 oz) crumbled blue cheese

1. Place potatoes in medium saucepan; cover with salted water. Bring to a boil; reduce heat and simmer about 15 minutes, or until tender. Place asparagus in steamer basket or strainer; set steamer on top of pot of simmering potatoes during last 5 minutes of cooking time.

2. Meanwhile, in medium serving bowl, whisk oil, vinegar, salt, and pepper until blended. Drain and halve potatoes (or quarter, if larger); immediately toss with vinaigrette, asparagus, scallions, and parsley. Crumble cheese on top; serve warm.

Corn on the Cob

6 ears corn, unhusked

1. In large pot of cold water, soak 6 ears corn, unhusked, for up to 1 hour. Drain, shaking off excess water.

2. Place on hot grill with steaks, grill about 18 minutes, until husks are charred and brown, turning several times.

3. Husk corn; serve 4 ears. Reserve remaining 2 ears for later use.

Nutritional Information

PER SERVING OF STEAK: 166 cal, 22 g protein, 8 g fat, 0 g carbohydrate, 62 mg cholesterol, 584 mg sodium

PER SERVING OF POTATO SALAD: 234 cal, 6 g protein, 14 g fat, 22 g carbohydrate, 11 mg cholesterol, 471 mg sodium

PER SERVING OF CORN: 72 cal, 2 g protein, 1 g fat, 17 g carbohydrate, 0 mg cholesterol, 3 mg sodium

Future Dinner: Lemon Chicken and Vegetables

An extra 10 minutes of grilling tonight gives you a head start on Monday, Wednesday, and Thursday nights' entrees. Grill the chicken and vegetables first, then cook Sunday's meal (above). After dinner, when everything has cooled, wrap and refrigerate.

8 boneless, skinless chicken-breast halves, marinated overnight in Lemon Marinade (pg. 166)
2 red onions, thickly sliced, marinated overnight in Lemon Marinade (pg. 166)
2 red bell peppers, halved and seeded
2 T bottled balsamic salad dressing

1. Preheat grill (high heat). Remove chicken and onion slices from marinade, reserving marinade. Grill chicken, onion, and peppers together. Grill chicken about 10 minutes, until just cooked through but still juicy, turning occasionally. Brush chicken with marinade in the first 5 minutes of grilling. Grill onion about 10 minutes, until tender and lightly charred, turning several times. Grill peppers about 10 minutes, until skin is blistered and charred, turning often.

2. Remove chicken and onion to cutting board to cool. Transfer peppers to a paper bag; let steam at least 10 minutes. Peel away charred skin, core and thinly slice. Coarsely chop onions. In large plastic container, combine pepper slices, onion, and salad dressing. Reserve chicken for later use.

TIMESAVING STRATEGIES

- Scrape kernels from reserved corn. Toss with pepper-onion mixture in plastic container; refrigerate to use Thursday.

- When reserved chicken is cool, refrigerate to use Monday and Wednesday.

- When reserved steak is cool, refrigerate to use Tuesday.

- Remove sandwich rolls from freezer on Monday morning; defrost, in resealable bag, at room temperature.

Blue-Ribbon Chicken Salad

Start by warming frozen rolls, then toss together the creamy chicken dish. Finish the meal with strawberries topped with whipped cream or ice cream.

4 large sandwich or French rolls
⅓ cup reduced-fat sour cream
⅓ cup reduced-fat mayonnaise
6 grilled chicken-breast halves (from
    Sunday), cut into ½-inch chunks
2 cucumbers, peeled, seeded, and sliced

½ cup pecans or walnuts, coarsely
    chopped
2 T chopped fresh dill
¾ tsp salt
¼ tsp black pepper
½ bag (16 oz) salad greens

1. Preheat oven or toaster oven to warm rolls.

2. In large serving bowl, whisk sour cream and mayonnaise until blended. Add remaining ingredients, except greens, and toss to combine. You'll use 6 of the chicken breast halves; save 2 for Wednesday.

3. Serve over greens with warmed rolls, or make into sandwiches.

Nutritional Information

PER SERVING: 376 cal, 44 g protein, 17 g fat, 13 g carbohydrate, 116 mg cholesterol, 740 mg sodium

Beefeaters' Steak Sandwiches

Leftover steak begs to be layered into a thick sandwich. Alter the amount of horseradish or the type of cheese according to your family's taste.

¼ cup reduced-fat mayonnaise
2 T prepared horseradish
8 slices pumpernickel
Grilled steak (reserved from Sunday), very thinly sliced
2 tomatoes, thinly sliced
¼ cup (2 oz) crumbled blue cheese
1 bunch watercress, trimmed

1. In a cup, combine mayonnaise and horseradish.

2. For each sandwich: Spread 1 side of bread slice with mayonnaise mixture. Layer steak slices, tomato, cheese, and watercress, then remaining bread slice.

Balsamic Green and Yellow Beans

If you like, you can cook the beans in advance, but wait to toss them with the dressing until just before serving; otherwise, the acid in the vinegar will leach the color from the beans.

½ lb fresh green beans, trimmed
½ lb fresh yellow beans, trimmed
2 T prepared balsamic salad dressing

1. Bring large pot of salted water to a boil over high heat. Cook beans together about 5 minutes, or until just tender; drain.

2. Toss with dressing.

Nutritional Information

PER SERVING OF SANDWICHES: 313 cal, 19 g protein, 10 g fat, 37 g carbohydrate, 39 mg cholesterol, 836 mg sodium

PER SERVING OF BEANS: 70 cal, 2 g protein, 4 g fat, 9 g carbohydrate, 0 mg cholesterol, 65 mg sodium

Chicken Pad Thai

In this basic Thai dish everything is simply sauteed together. Thai fish sauce is found in the Asian section of your supermarket. If unavailable, substitute soy sauce.

1 pkg (8 oz) rice stick noodles
3 T olive oil
4 scallions, thinly sliced, both white and green parts
2 cloves garlic, chopped
¼ cup fresh lime juice (reserved from Saturday)
3 T Thai fish sauce or soy sauce
2 T granulated sugar

¼ tsp red-pepper flakes (optional)
2 grilled chicken-breast halves (reserved from Sunday), thinly sliced
2 T Peanut-Sesame Sauce (reserved from Saturday)
2 T Lime-Cilantro Sauce (reserved from Saturday)
1 cup (4 oz) mung-bean sprouts (optional)

1. In large bowl, soak noodles in warm water at least 20 minutes. Drain.

2. Warm oil in wok or large deep skillet over medium-high heat. Add scallions (reserve some green slices for garnish) and garlic; stir-fry 30 seconds. Add lime juice, fish sauce, sugar, and pepper flakes. Increase heat to high; stir-fry 1 minute.

3. Stir in chicken, then soaked noodles and both sauces. Cook 3 minutes, stirring until chicken is warm and sauce is completely incorporated. Transfer to serving bowl. Toss with sprouts; garnish with reserved scallion greens.

Nutritional Information

PER SERVING: 337 cal, 9 g protein, 25 g fat, 21 g carbohydrate, 18 mg cholesterol, 117 mg sodium

Grilled-Vegetable Wraps

If the kids prefer their wraps stuffed only with cheese, the extra veggies make a terrific sandwich filler for tomorrow's brown-bag lunch. Round out the meal with the remaining green salad tossed with bottled dressing.

1 pkg (3½ oz) boil-in-bag long-grain rice
Grilled vegetables (reserved from Sunday)
¼ cup chopped fresh Italian parsley
1 cup (4 oz) shredded Jarlsberg or Swiss cheese
4 large flour tortillas

1. Preheat oven to 350°F. Prepare rice according to package directions. Meanwhile, in medium bowl, toss vegetables with parsley.

2. For each wrap: Place ½ cup rice in middle of each tortilla, top with 1 cup vegetable mixture, then ¼ cup cheese. Fold in at top and bottom, then roll up sides. Wrap each in foil; bake 15 minutes, or until warmed through.

Nutritional Information

PER SERVING: 590 cal, 20 g protein, 16 g fat, 90 g carbohydrate, 25 mg cholesterol, 616 mg sodium

Peanut-Sesame Noodles

Make this Chinese-restaurant staple at home using the rest of the reserved sauces. For flavor and nutrition, we've thrown in crunchy snow peas, but frozen green peas would work as well.

12–16 oz vermicelli or linguine
½ lb fresh snow peas, trimmed
¾ cup Peanut-Sesame Sauce (reserved from Saturday)
2 T Lime-Cilantro Sauce (reserved from Saturday)
1 tsp Asian sesame oil
½ tsp salt

1. Cook pasta according to package directions, adding peas in last minute of cooking time. Drain, reserving ¼ cup cooking water.

2. In large serving bowl, combine sauces, sesame oil, salt, and reserved pasta water. Add pasta and peas; toss to combine. Serve warm or cold.

Cool Cucumber Salad

Cucumber seeds are sometimes bitter. To remove them, halve cucumber lengthwise, then use the tip of a teaspoon to scrape out the seeds.

¼ cup rice-wine vinegar
1 T granulated sugar
2 large cucumbers, peeled, seeded, and thinly sliced
½ red onion, thinly sliced and broken into rings
2 T chopped fresh dill

In large serving bowl, whisk vinegar, sugar, and 2 T water until sugar dissolves. Add cucumber, onion, and dill; toss to combine. Serve immediately.

Nutritional Information

PER SERVING OF NOODLES: 330 cal, 11 g protein, 19 g fat, 31 g carbohydrate, 0 mg cholesterol, 536 mg sodium
PER SERVING OF SALAD: 39 cal, 1 g protein, trace fat, 9 g carbohydrate, 0 mg cholesterol, 4 mg sodium

Summer Treats with Saucy Sauces

You'll make three different flavor-packed dressings on Saturday: A lemony dressing is used as a marinade for Saturday's grilled salmon and Monday's grilled chicken, and a sauce in Wednesday's couscous. Sunday's London Broil provides meat for Tuesday's sandwiches. The extra grilled vegetables are transformed in Wednesday couscous. Thursday's tacos and gazpacho are both easy to make. On Friday, Thursday's soup is paired with a few vegetables and a can of tuna for a pasta sauce that practically prepares itself.

MENU

Saturday
Summer-Thyme Salmon
Corn on the Cob
Cherry Tomatoes

Sunday
Balsamic London Broil and Grilled Vegetables
Grilled or Toasted Italian Bread

Monday
Grilled-Chicken Cobb Salad
Toasted Whole-Wheat Rolls

Tuesday
Asian Steak Sandwiches
Celery–Red Pepper Salad

Wednesday
Couscous Salad with Grilled Vegetables
Toasted Mini Pitas

Thursday
Black-Bean and Turkey Tacos
Garden Gazpacho

Friday
Pasta Salad Niçoise
Warm Breadsticks

Produce
5 large lemons
3 large limes
1 large head Romaine lettuce
1 large head green-leaf lettuce
1 bunch fresh parsley
1 bunch fresh thyme
1 bunch fresh cilantro
1 bunch scallions (You'll need 6.)
1 medium cucumber
3 medium zucchini
3 medium yellow squash
1 medium eggplant
5 medium red peppers
1 bunch celery
4 medium ears fresh corn
5 medium tomatoes
1 pint cherry tomatoes
½ lb green beans
1 large avocado
3 large red onions
1 head garlic

Bread/Starches
2 loaves Italian bread (each about 12 inches long)
4 whole-wheat rolls
1 pkg mini pita pockets
1 box couscous (10 oz)
1 pkg taco shells (12 shells)
Penne or bow-tie pasta (You'll need 8 oz.)

Canned/Packaged
1 can (6 oz) water-pack tuna
1 can (15 oz) chickpeas
1 can (15 oz) black beans
1 bottle (10 oz) low-sodium vegetable juice cocktail

1 can (13¾ oz) reduced-sodium chicken broth
Reduced-fat blue cheese dressing (You'll need ½ cup.)

Meat/Fish
1 salmon fillet, about 1 inch at thickest part (about 1½ lb)
4 boneless, skinless chicken-breast halves
1 London broil, about 1¼ inches thick (about 1½ lb)
1 pkg (5.5 oz) vacuum-packed, oven-roasted turkey-breast slices
Bacon (You'll need 4 strips.)

Dairy /Freezer
1 pkg (4 oz) crumbled feta cheese
1 pkg (4 oz) shredded cheddar cheese
1 container (8 oz) nonfat sour cream
1 tube refrigerated breadsticks
Large eggs (You'll need 2.)

Staples
Olive oil
Balsamic vinegar
Dijon mustard
Reduced-sodium soy sauce
Ground cumin
Sugar
Salt and black pepper
Aluminum foil, plastic wrap, and large resealable plastic bags

Desserts
Your choice!

After shopping, Saturday is prep day. First you'll make the special sauces, then you'll get a jump on the rest of the week

Lemon-Thyme Marinade

From 4 lemons, grate 1 T peel and squeeze the juice. From 2 limes, grate ½ tsp peel and squeeze the juice. Refrigerate separately, to use Saturday and Thursday. To make Lemon-Thyme Marinade:

⅔ cup olive oil
1 T grated lemon peel
½ cup fresh lemon juice
2 T chopped fresh thyme, or 2 tsp dried thyme
½ tsp salt
½ tsp black pepper

In small jar with tight-fitting lid, shake all ingredients until blended. Refrigerate until ready to use.

YIELD: ABOUT 1¼ CUPS

Balsamic Marinade

½ cup olive oil
⅓ cup balsamic vinegar
2 T Dijon mustard
2 large cloves garlic, minced
½ tsp salt
½ tsp black pepper

In small jar with tight-fitting lid, shake all ingredients until blended. Refrigerate until ready to use.

YIELD: ABOUT 1 CUP

Asian Dressing

3 T olive oil
3 T reduced-sodium soy sauce
½ tsp grated lime peel
2 T fresh lime juice
1 clove garlic, minced
1 tsp sugar
1 tsp Dijon mustard

In small jar with tight-fitting lid, shake all ingredients until blended. Refrigerate until ready to use.

YIELD: ABOUT ½ CUP

TIME SAVING STRATEGIES

- Marinate London broil in ½ cup of the Balsamic Marinade (see Sunday's recipe, step 1). Refrigerate to use Sunday.

- Split Italian bread lengthwise (see grocery list), then quarter and hollow out. Freeze in resealable plastic bag to use Tuesday.

Summer-Thyme Salmon

While you're grilling Saturday's savory main dish of Summer-Thyme Salmon, cook the chicken for Monday's supper.

1 salmon fillet, about 1 inch at thickest part (about 1½ lb)
4 boneless, skinless chicken-breast halves, pounded to ½-inch thickness
⅔ cup Lemon-Thyme Marinade (See recipe pg. 181)
1 lemon, cut in wedges

1. Rinse salmon and chicken and pat dry; place in separate resealable plastic bags. Add ⅓ cup of the marinade to each bag; flip bags to coat salmon and chicken. Refrigerate for 30 minutes to 1 hour. The unused marinade is refrigerated until Wednesday's dinner.

2. Meanwhile, prepare grill (high heat). Position lightly greased grill rack about 4 inches from heat. Place salmon, skin side down, and chicken on grill. Brush each with marinade from bags (don't mix marinades). Cover with grill lid and cook for 4 minutes.

3. Turn chicken (don't turn fish). Cover; cook 5 to 7 minutes longer, until fish is tender and flakes with fork, and chicken is just cooked through.

4. Using two metal spatulas, remove salmon and chicken from grill. (Refrigerate chicken for later use.) Serve salmon with lemon wedges. When chicken is cool, wrap well and refrigerate for use on Monday.

Nutritional Information

PER SERVING OF SALMON: 371 cal, 39 g protein, 27 g fat, 1 g carbohydrate, 102 mg cholesterol, 169 mg sodium

Balsamic London Broil and Grilled Vegetables

Use the same full-flavored marinade to season the steak and the vegetables. If your family doesn't care for one of the vegetables, simply omit and use more of the other vegetables.

London Broil

1½ lb London broil, about 1¼ inches thick
½ cup Balsamic Marinade (reserved from Saturday)

Grilled Vegetables

3 zucchini, sliced lengthwise about ¼ inch thick
3 yellow squash, sliced lengthwise about ¼ inch thick
3 red and/or yellow peppers, quartered
3 red onions, cut into ¼-inch-thick rounds or wedges
1 eggplant, sliced lengthwise about ½ inch thick
½ cup Balsamic Marinade (reserved from Saturday)

1. In large resealable plastic bag, combine meat and marinade; flip bag to coat meat. Refrigerate at least 2 hours or overnight. About 30 minutes before grilling, remove marinated meat from refrigerator.

2. Meanwhile, prepare grill (high heat). Position grill rack about 4 inches from heat. Place meat on grill; brush with marinade from bag. Cook for 14 to 16 minutes, turning once, until medium rare or of desired doneness. Remove meat to cutting board; cover with foil and let rest about 10 minutes.

3. While steak rests, grill vegetables for 10 minutes, turning once and brushing often with marinade, until tender-crisp. (Grill in 2 batches if necessary.) Set aside half of vegetables (refrigerate for later use). Place remaining vegetables on serving platter.

4. Cut steak in half (refrigerate 1 portion for later use). Thinly slice remaining steak and serve with grilled vegetables.

 TIMESAVING STRATEGIES

- When reserved vegetables are cool, refrigerate to use Wednesday and Thursday.

- When reserved steak is cool, refrigerate to use Tuesday.

Nutritional Information

PER SERVING OF STEAK: 253 cal, 20 g protein, 18 g fat, 1 g carbohydrate, 58 mg cholesterol, 226 mg sodium

PER SERVING OF VEGETABLES: 116 cal, 3 g protein, 7 g fat, 13 g carbohydrate, 0 mg cholesterol, 98 mg sodium

Grilled-Chicken Cobb Salad

You can assemble this classic California salad in no time since the chicken is already cooked. For hard-cooking eggs: Cover the eggs in a saucepan with cold water and bring to a boil. Immediately remove from heat; let stand for 10 minutes, then run under cold water to cool slightly.

1 head green leaf lettuce, shredded (about 8 cups)
Grilled chicken-breast halves (reserved from Saturday), thinly sliced
2 hard-cooked eggs, chopped
2 tomatoes, chopped
½ ripe avocado, thinly sliced
4 slices bacon, cooked and crumbled
½ cup bottled reduced-fat blue cheese dressing

Place shredded lettuce on serving platter. Top with rows of chicken slices, eggs, tomatoes, and avocado. Sprinkle with bacon. Serve with dressing.

TIMESAVING STRATEGIES

- Sprinkle 1 T fresh lemon juice over remaining avocado half. Press plastic wrap directly on surface of avocado and refrigerate to use Tuesday.

- Remove Italian bread from freezer Tuesday morning; defrost in resealable bag at room temperature.

Nutritional Information

PER SERVING: 427 cal, 36 g protein, 27 g fat, 11 g carbohydrate, 184 mg cholesterol, 669 mg sodium

Asian Steak Sandwiches

Italian bread (frozen Saturday)
Balsamic London broil (reserved from Sunday), thinly sliced
2 scallions, thinly sliced
Asian dressing (reserved from Saturday)
4 leaves Romaine lettuce
½ ripe avocado (reserved from Monday), thinly sliced

1. In medium bowl, toss together steak slices, scallions, and ½ of the dressing.

2. Toast bread; brush with dressing. Assemble sandwiches.

Celery–Red Pepper Salad

3 stalks celery, cut into thin strips
1 red pepper, cut into thin strips
¼ cup torn cilantro leaves
½ tsp sugar
¼ tsp salt
¼ tsp black pepper

Toss all ingredients. Let stand for 15 minutes. Enjoy!

Nutritional Information

PER SERVING OF SANDWICH: 502 cal, 21 g protein, 30 g fat, 36 g carbohydrate, 44 mg cholesterol, 991 mg sodium
PER SERVING OF SALAD: 12 cal, trace protein, 1 g fat, 3 g carbohydrate, 0 mg cholesterol, 160 mg sodium

Couscous Salad with Grilled Vegetables

Tempt your family on a hot day with this healthful main-dish salad.

1 box (10 oz) couscous
1 can (10½–13¾ oz) reduced-sodium chicken broth
Lemon-Thyme Marinade (from Saturday)
1 clove garlic, crushed
½ tsp ground cumin
Grilled vegetables (from Sunday)
1 can (10–19 oz) chickpeas, drained and rinsed
3 T chopped fresh parsley
8 leaves Romaine lettuce
1 pkg (4 oz) crumbled feta cheese

1. Cook couscous according to package directions, combining chicken broth with enough water to equal the amount of liquid specified on package (omit salt or butter). Place cooked couscous in large bowl to cool; fluff with fork.

2. To the marinade in jar, add garlic and cumin; shake until blended. Drizzle over cooled couscous; toss to coat.

3. Remove 5 pieces of grilled red onion (refrigerate for later use). Chop remaining vegetables, then add to couscous with chickpeas and parsley. Toss well. Spoon mixture onto lettuce-lined platter; sprinkle with feta cheese.

Nutritional Information

PER SERVING: 814 cal, 24 g protein, 40 g fat, 93 g carbohydrate, 25 mg cholesterol, 638 mg sodium

Black-Bean and Turkey Tacos

This meal comes together in a snap: Blend lots of summer produce for the refreshing gazpacho, then warm the shells and toss together the no-cook ingredients for the crunchy tacos.

2 T fresh lime juice (reserved from Saturday)
2 T chopped fresh cilantro
½ tsp ground cumin
½ tsp salt
1 can (15–19 oz) black beans, drained and rinsed
1 pkg (5.5 oz) vacuum-packed oven-roasted turkey-breast slices, diced
2 scallions, chopped
1 stalk celery, diced
1 pkg (12 shells) taco shells
Remaining Romaine lettuce, finely shredded (about 3 cups)
½ container (8-oz size) nonfat sour cream
1 pkg (4 oz) shredded cheddar cheese

1. In large bowl, whisk together first 4 ingredients. Stir in beans, turkey, scallions, and celery.

2. Warm taco shells according to package directions.

3. To assemble: Divide lettuce among shells; top with bean mixture, sour cream, then cheese. (Refrigerate remaining sour cream for later use.)

Garden Gazpacho

This summer classic does involve some chopping. If you have the energy, make it on Tuesday night, and refrigerate in a plastic container until Thursday.

3 tomatoes, quartered
2 stalks celery, coarsely chopped
1 red pepper, coarsely chopped
1 cucumber, peeled, seeded, and coarsely chopped
Grilled red-onion rounds or wedges (reserved from Wednesday), coarsely chopped
1 small clove garlic, crushed
1 bottle (10 oz) low-sodium vegetable-juice cocktail
2 T olive oil
1 T balsamic vinegar
½ tsp salt
¼ tsp black pepper
1 lime, cut into wedges

1. In food processor fitted with metal blade, process all ingredients, pulsing, until mixture becomes soupy, but vegetables are still slightly chunky. (Process in batches if necessary.)

2. Remove 1¼ cups soup (refrigerate for later use). Refrigerate remaining soup for at least 30 minutes for best flavor. Serve with lime wedges.

 TIMESAVING STRATEGIES

- Refrigerate remaining sour cream to use Friday.
- Refrigerate reserved gazpacho to use Friday.

Nutritional Information

PER SERVING OF TACO: 144 cal, 9 g protein, 7 g fat, 15 g carbohydrate, 16 mg cholesterol, 337 mg sodium
PER SERVING OF GAZPACHO: 97 cal, 2 g protein, 6 g fat, 11 g carbohydrate, 0 mg cholesterol, 250 mg sodium

Pasta Salad Niçoise

Wrap up the week with a family-pleasing pasta dish. Toss tuna, penne, and bright green beans with a creamy tomato sauce. Get the kids to help in baking the refrigerated prepared breadsticks—they love popping open the can.

8 oz penne or bow-tie pasta
½ lb green beans, halved
Garden Gazpacho (reserved from Thursday)
1 can (6 oz) water-packed tuna, drained and flaked
2 scallions, chopped
½ container (8-oz size) nonfat sour cream
2–3 T chopped fresh parsley
2 tsp chopped fresh thyme, or ½ tsp dried thyme
½ tsp salt
¼ tsp black pepper

1. Cook pasta according to package directions, adding green beans to the pot during the last 2 minutes of cooking. Drain; rinse pasta and beans well in cold water.

2. In large bowl, combine remaining ingredients. Stir in pasta and beans.

Nutritional Information

PER SERVING: 196 cal, 18 g protein, 2 g fat, 27 g carbohydrate, 14 mg cholesterol, 243 mg sodium

Pennsylvania-Dutch Treat

On Saturday, braised chicken is served with a savory fruit sauce. Some of that sauce is then used to stuff Sunday's pan-seared pork chops. Extra cooked pork chops are the starting point for Tuesday's Southern-inspired black-eyed peas. The extra braised chicken turns up in Monday's diner-style sandwiches and Wednesday's creamy casserole. On Thursday, there's ham-and-cheese strata. Friday features a white bean stew and crisp focaccia.

MENU

Saturday
Cider-Braised Chicken
Long-Grain Rice
Green Salad with Seasoned Croutons

Sunday
Stuffed Pork Chops with Fall Fruits
Creamed Spinach

Monday
Chicken Skillet Sandwiches
Diner Tomato Soup

Tuesday
Black-Eyed Peas with Pork and Sautéed Greens
Bakery Biscuits or Cornbread

Wednesday
Lancaster County Casserole
Green Salad

Thursday
Ham and Cheese Strata
Green Salad
Fresh Fruit

Friday
Hearty White-Bean Ragout
Fast Focaccia

GROCERY LIST FOR THE WEEK

Produce
2 large lemons
Fresh fruit of your choice
2 Granny Smith or other tart apple
1 bag (10 oz) precleaned salad greens
1 bag (16 oz) precleaned salad greens
1 bunch fresh thyme
1 large bunch kale or collard greens
1 bunch fresh Italian parsley
1 pint cherry tomatoes
1 bunch celery
1 head garlic
4 medium onions

Meat/Fish
5 lb bone-in chicken pieces (1 whole
    fryer chicken plus 4 breast
    halves), skinned
6 boneless pork chops, about 1 inch
    thick (about 4 oz each)

Frozen
2 pkg (10-oz size) frozen chopped
    spinach
1 pkg (10 oz) frozen peas

Dairy/Deli
Butter (You'll need 2 T.)
2 quarts low-fat milk
1 block (4 oz) Parmesan cheese
1 bag (8 oz) shredded cheddar cheese
8 oz cooked deli ham, thinly sliced
4 oz Swiss cheese, sliced
Large eggs (You'll need 4.)

Bread
4 bakery biscuits or cornbread pieces
1 loaf whole-wheat or white bread
    (You'll need 16 slices.)

1 large (12 inch) prebaked pizza
    crust

Packaged
1 box (8 oz) mixed dried fruit
Apple cider (You'll need 3½ cups.)
1 box (about 6 oz) seasoned rice mix,
    or long-grain rice
1 box (about 5 oz) seasoned croutons
Dried bread crumbs (You'll need
    about ¼ cup.)
2 cans (10-oz size) tomato soup
2 cans (15-oz size) black-eyed peas
2 cans (15-oz size) small white or
    cannelloni beans
1 can (13¾-oz size) reduced-sodium
    chicken broth
1 box (8 oz) wide egg noodles
2 cans (10¾-oz size) cream of roasted
    chicken with savory herbs soup,
    or cream of chicken
1 can (15 oz) whole tomatoes

Staples
Olive oil
Prepared salad dressing
Vegetable cooking spray
All-purpose flour
Light-brown sugar
Balsamic vinegar
Ground nutmeg
Dijon or German-style mustard
Reduced-fat mayonnaise
Hot pepper sauce
Salt and black pepper
Aluminum foil, plastic wrap, and re-
    sealable plastic bags

Cider-Braised Chicken

When meat is braised, it's browned in the skillet first, then simmered in a small amount of liquid, in this case, apple cider. The browning step is important, as it adds a huge amount of richness and flavor. We recommend buying 1 whole chicken plus 4 extra breasts, so there's plenty of white meat to use in later meals. Have the butcher skin it for you. Cook up some plain rice, or a seasoned rice dish on the side, and toss a bag of salad greens with your favorite prepared dressing and handful of packaged seasoned croutons.

5 lb bone-in chicken pieces (about 12 pieces), skinned
1 tsp salt
½ tsp black pepper, optional
2 T olive oil
2 medium onions, cut into chunks
2 Granny Smith or other tart apple, unpeeled and cut into ½-inch chunks

3 cloves garlic, chopped
1 pkg (8 oz) mixed dried fruit
2 T fresh lemon juice (from ½ lemon)
1 T thyme leaves
2 cups apple cider
2 T fresh Italian parsley, optional garnish

1. Preheat oven to 400°F. Wash and pat dry chicken; season with salt and pepper.

2. Warm oil in large Dutch oven over medium-high heat. Add chicken; brown in 3 batches until browned on all sides, about 4 minutes per side, turning with tongs. Set aside.

3. To same pot over medium-high heat, add ½ cup water; stirring to loosen browned bits. Bring water to a simmer; add onions. Cover and simmer 5 minutes. Add apples, dried fruit, garlic, lemon juice, and thyme. Cook 10 minutes, until fruit is tender. Add chicken and cider. Cover pot; place in oven and braise 25 minutes, or until chicken is cooked through and apples are tender.

4. Remove pot from oven; transfer chicken to serving platter. Place pot over medium-high heat and bring sauce to a simmer. Let simmer about 5 minutes

• • •

Penne with Broccoli and Double Tomato Sauce (p.146)

· · ·

Blue-Ribbon Chicken Salad (p.172)

Shrimp Fajitas with Mango-Lime Salsa (p.167)

• • •

Peanut-Sesame Noodles (p.177)

Chicken Pad Thai (p.175)

Grilled-Vegetable Wraps (p. 176)

• • •

Steak au Poivre (p. 28)

· · ·

Beefeaters Steak Sandwich (left);
Balsamic Green Beans (right) (p.173)

• • •

Fresh Tuna Salad Nicoise (p.24)

• • •

Cider-Braised Chicken with Long-Grain Rice (front) (p. 194) Lancaster
County Casserole (left) and Green Salad (right) (p. 200)

Black-eyed Peas with Pork and
Sautéed Greens (front) (p. 199); Diner
Tomato Soup (left); Chicken Skillet
Sandwiches (back) (p. 198)

• • •

Stuffed Pork Chops with Fall Fruits and Creamed Spinach (front) (p.196);
Hearty White-Bean Ragout (back) (p.203)

· · ·

Puff-Pastry Turkey Pie (p.217)

· · ·

Pumpkin-Walnut Rigatoni (back); Spinach Salad with Bacon Bits (right) (p.221);
Puff-Pastry Turkey Pie (front) (p.217)

• • •

Holiday Feasting: Roast Turkey (left); Mashed Potatoes (from left) Leeks and Herbed Bread Stuffing;
Cranberry Sauce; Brown-Sugar Glazed Butternut Squash; Confetti Succotash (back) (p. 208)

. . .
Petal Phyllo Cream Cup
Garnished with Mixed Berries (p. 232)

to reduce sauce. Reserve ¼ cup of fruit sauce for later use. Reserve 4 breast halves for later use. Serve remaining chicken drizzled with remaining fruit sauce; sprinkle with parsley, if desired.

 TIMESAVING STRATEGIES

- Refrigerate reserved 4 breast halves in resealable plastic bags to use Monday and Wednesday.
- Refrigerate reserved ¼ cup fruit sauce to use Sunday.
- Reserve ½ cup croutons to use on Monday.
- Refrigerate remaining apple cider to use Sunday.

Nutritional Information

PER SERVING: 595 cal, 67 g protein, 20 g fat, 34 g carbohydrate, 200 mg cholesterol, 735 mg sodium

Stuffed Pork Chops with Fall Fruits

Just a bit of the sweet-tart fruit sauce adds a burst of flavor to these mild pork chops. Of course, you can leave the filling out if your family prefers. Remember to cook two extra, unstuffed chops for Tuesday's salad. If all the chops don't fit in 1 skillet, use 2 smaller skillets and divide the cider. Cook the spinach dish while the pork simmers.

6 boneless pork chops, 1 inch thick (about 5 oz each)
4 T fruit sauce (reserved from Saturday)
½ tsp salt
¼ tsp black pepper
2 T olive oil
1½ cups apple cider

1. Using a small sharp knife, cut horizontal 2-inch slits through 4 of the chops to form a deep pocket. (Leave 2 chops unstuffed). Stuff pockets with equal amounts of apple mixture. Sprinkle chops with salt and pepper.

2. Warm oil in large skillet over medium-high heat until hot. Brown chops about 3 minutes per side. Add cider; cover, reduce heat, and simmer 12 minutes, until just cooked through. Remove chops to serving platter.

3. Over high heat, simmer pan juices for about 8 minutes, until reduced to about ¾ cup. Reserve 2 unstuffed chops for later use. Serve 4 remaining chops drizzled with pan sauce.

Creamed Spinach

2 pkg (10 oz) frozen chopped spinach
2 T butter
½ medium onion, finely chopped
2 T all-purpose flour
1½ cups low-fat milk
Salt and pepper
Ground nutmeg
¼ cup grated Parmesan cheese

1. Thaw spinach in microwave; squeeze out excess water.

2. Warm butter in large skillet over medium heat. Sauté onion for 2 minutes, or until soft, stirring frequently.

3. Stir in flour and cook 1 minute, until flour is lightly browned. Increase heat to medium-high; slowly add milk and stir until sauce is thick and boiling.

4. Stir in spinach and add salt, pepper, and ground nutmeg to taste. Reduce heat to low, cover and cook 4 minutes longer, until spinach is tender. Stir in ¼ cup Parmesan cheese and serve hot.

 TIMESAVING STRATEGIES

- Refrigerate 2 unstuffed pork chops, tightly wrapped, to use Tuesday.

- Refrigerate ½ medium onion, tightly wrapped, to use Tuesday.

Nutritional Information

PER SERVING OF PORK: 256 cal, 18 g protein, 15 g fat, 12 g carbohydrate, 58 mg cholesterol, 311 mg sodium

PER SERVING OF SPINACH: 171 cal, 11 g protein, 9 g fat, 15 g carbohydrate, 24 mg cholesterol, 285 mg sodium

Chicken Skillet Sandwiches

Soup and sandwiches are the perfect ready-in-10-minutes dinner.

8 slices whole-wheat or white bread
2 tsp Dijon or German-style mustard, or to taste
4 slices (about 2 oz) cooked deli ham
¾ cup shredded cheddar cheese
2 braised chicken-breast halves (reserved from Saturday), thinly sliced
¼ cup reduced-fat mayonnaise

1. On each of 4 bread slices, layer mustard, ham, cheese, and chicken slices; top with remaining bread slices. Spread mayonnaise on outside of sandwiches.

2. Warm large, nonstick skillet over medium heat. Cook sandwiches 2 to 3 minutes per side, lightly pressing down on sandwiches with a spatula.

Diner Tomato Soup

Prepare 2 cans (10-oz size) tomato soup according to package directions. Serve with croutons and ¼ cup shredded cheddar cheese, if desired.

Nutritional Information

PER SERVING OF SANDWICH: 280 cal, 26 g protein, 10 g fat, 24 g carbohydrate, 70 mg cholesterol, 801 mg sodium
PER SERVING OF SOUP: 100 cal, 2 g protein, 1 g fat, 22 g carbohydrate, trace cholesterol, 760 mg sodium

Black-Eyed Peas with Pork and Greens

We love the combination of pork, black-eyed peas, and dark, leafy kale. Warm biscuits in toaster oven.

1 large bunch kale or collard greens, trimmed and coarsely chopped
2 tsp light-brown sugar
¾ tsp salt, divided
1 T olive oil
2 stalks celery, thinly sliced
½ medium onion, thinly sliced (reserved from Sunday)
2 tsp fresh thyme leaves
2 cans (15-oz size) black-eyed peas, drained and rinsed
2 pork chops (reserved from Sunday), thinly sliced
½ cup reduced-sodium chicken broth
2 T fresh lemon juice (from 1 lemon)
2 T chopped fresh Italian parsley
¼ tsp hot pepper sauce
Pinch black pepper

1. Bring large pot of salted water to a boil over high heat. Add greens; cook 10 minutes, until tender. Drain. In medium serving bowl, toss kale with brown sugar and ½ tsp of salt.

2. Meanwhile, warm oil in large skillet over medium-low heat. Add celery, onion, and thyme; cook 7 minutes, stirring often until vegetables are softened. Add beans, pork slices, broth, lemon juice, parsley, pepper sauce, black pepper, and the remaining ¼ tsp salt; cook 5 minutes to absorb liquids and warm through. Transfer to large serving bowl; serve with warm kale. Reserve leftover chicken broth in can for Friday.

Nutritional Information

PER SERVING: 289 cal, 17 g protein, 14 g fat, 24 g carbohydrate, 36 mg cholesterol, 460 mg sodium

Lancaster County Casserole

This casserole, a homey, old-fashioned dish, freezes well, so if you're feeling really ambitious, double the recipe and make two. Freeze one casserole before baking. (Remember to add needed ingredients to the shopping list.)

1 box (8 oz) wide egg noodles
2 cans (10¾-oz size) cream of roasted
  chicken with savory herbs soup or
  cream of chicken soup
1 cup low-fat milk
1 whole roasted chicken breast (reserved
  from Saturday), cut into small
  chunks

1 pkg (10 oz) frozen peas
½ tsp salt
¼ tsp black pepper
1 cup (4 oz) shredded cheddar cheese
¼ cup plain dried bread crumbs

1. Preheat oven to 350°F. Cook noodles according to package directions; drain. Meanwhile, in small saucepan over medium heat, combine both cans of soup and milk. Warm 3 minutes, stirring to blend.

2. Grease a shallow 10-inch casserole or baking dish. In large mixing bowl, combine noodles, chicken chunks, soup mixture, peas, salt, and pepper; spoon into prepared baking dish. Top with cheese and bread crumbs. Cover with lid or foil; bake 20 minutes.

3. Uncover; bake 20 minutes longer or until hot and bubbly.

Nutritional Information

PER SERVING: 507 cal, 34 g protein, 22 g fat, 43 g carbohydrate, 100 mg cholesterol, 1823 mg sodium

Green Salad

Toss half of a (16 oz) bag of salad greens with ½ pint of cherry tomatoes and prepared dressing.

 TIMESAVING STRATEGIES

- Refrigerate remaining half bag of salad greens to use Thursday.
- Reserve remaining cherry tomatoes at room temperature to use Thursday.

Ham-and-Cheese Strata

This is really just a fun and fancy way to serve ham-and-cheese sandwiches. Make it a compete meal by adding a salad and whatever fruit is in season.

8 slices whole-wheat or white bread
8 slices (about 6 oz) cooked deli ham
4 thin slices (4 oz) Swiss cheese
½ pint cherry tomatoes, halved
4 large eggs
½ tsp salt
¼ tsp black pepper
2 cups low-fat milk

1. **Grease** a 9- by 13-inch baking dish. Make 4 sandwiches with bread, ham, and cheese. Remove crusts and cut sandwiches in half diagonally to make 8 triangles. Arrange sandwich triangles in a single row down the length of the pan, point up, one overlapping the other, so they fit snugly in the pan. Fit tomato halves to the left and right of the sandwich halves. Preheat oven to 350°F.

2. **In medium bowl,** whisk eggs, salt, and pepper. Gradually whisk in milk. Pour mixture over sandwiches and let stand 15 minutes at room temperature.

3. **Bake** strata 35 minutes, until top is lightly browned and custard just set. Cool slightly before serving.

Nutritional Information

PER SERVING: 471 cal, 34 g protein, 19 g fat, 43 g carbohydrate, 263 mg cholesterol, 1445 mg sodium

Hearty White-Bean Ragout

We like this served thick and rich—but if you prefer, add water for a thinner stew. Leftovers make a great pasta sauce, or can be frozen for a future dinner.

1 T olive oil
1 medium onion, coarsely chopped
2 stalks celery, sliced
4 cloves garlic, chopped
1 T fresh thyme leaves
2 cans (15 oz) white beans, drained (½ cup draining liquid reserved)
1 can (15 oz) whole tomatoes
¾ cup reduced-sodium chicken broth (reserved from Saturday)
1 T balsamic vinegar
½ tsp salt
¼ tsp black pepper

1. Warm oil in medium Dutch oven over medium-low heat. Add onion and celery; cook 7 minutes, stirring. Add garlic and thyme; cook 1 minute, stirring.

2. Add beans and reserved liquid, tomatoes, broth, vinegar, salt, and pepper; stir gently. Increase heat to high; bring to a simmer. Reduce heat; simmer 5 minutes, to allow flavors to blend, breaking up tomatoes with a wooden spoon.

3. Ladle into soup bowls and serve hot.

Fast Focaccia

Large (12 inch) prepared pizza crust
2 tsp olive oil
2 cloves garlic, minced (optional)
½ cup grated Parmesan cheese

1. Preheat oven to 450°F. Place pizza crust on ungreased baking sheet. Drizzle with olive oil. Sprinkle on garlic and Parmesan cheese.

2. Bake about 8 minutes, until slightly crisp. Cut into wedges and serve hot.

Nutritional Information

PER SERVING OF STEW: 112 cal, 7 g protein, 3 g fat, 19 g carbohydrate, 0 mg cholesterol, 491 mg sodium

PER SERVING OF FOCACCIA: 302 cal, 13 g protein, 9 g fat, 41 g carbohydrate, 10 mg cholesterol, 803 mg sodium

Holiday Feasting: Thanksgiving and Beyond

Thanksgiving leftovers are tasty but we realize that you can't eat turkey sandwiches for four days running, so we've come up with a plan for a week of unique and creative dinners that flow from one Thanksgiving night.

Two of the week's meals are freezeable. They'll come in handy during the hectic month ahead.

The feast itself includes many traditional side-dish favorites. We decided not to ask you to reserve any bread stuffing or mashed potatoes for later use. For the rest of the sides, you purposely make (or buy, in the case of the cranberry sauce) extra to form a foundation for the coming week.

MENU

Thanksgiving Dinner
Roast Turkey
Leek and Herbed Bread Stuffing
Confetti Succotash
Brown-Sugar Glazed Butternut Squash
Sour Cream Mashed Potatoes
Plus: prepared cranberry sauce (*no recipe given*); green salad; and dinner rolls

Friday
Lazy Leftover Sandwiches
Autumn Squash Soup

Saturday
Loaded Potato Skins
Big Green Salad

Sunday
Wild Rice and Turkey Salad with Cranberries
Swiss Cheese Rolls

Monday
Pumpkin-Walnut Rigatoni
Spinach Salad with Bacon Bits

Future Night
Puff-Pastry Turkey Pie
Green Salad

Future Night
Turkey and Wild Rice Soup

Produce
1 bunch celery
1 bunch leeks (4 stalks)
1 bunch fresh Italian parsley
1 large bunch fresh thyme
1 bunch fresh sage
1 bunch fresh chives
1 lb fresh green beans
3 large shallots
4 butternut squash (1¼ lb each)
10 large russet potatoes (about 5½ lb)
1 bunch scallions
1 bag (10 oz) precleaned salad greens, plus enough for Thanksgiving dinner
1 bag (8 oz) baby spinach leaves, or 1 bag (10 oz) fresh spinach

Meat
1 16-lb whole turkey
1 lb sliced bacon

Packaged Goods
1 jar (10–12 oz) turkey gravy
4 cans (13¾ oz) reduced-sodium chicken broth
1 pkg (12–16 oz) bread stuffing mix
1 bag (10 oz) cups walnuts
1 can (15 oz) solid-pack pumpkin
2 boxes (8-oz size) wild-rice blend
1 bottle balsamic salad dressing
1 can (8 oz) cranberry sauce, plus enough for Thanksgiving dinner
1 box (16 oz) rigatoni

Dairy
1 lb butter
1 cup whole milk
1 bag (8 oz) shredded cheddar cheese
1 bag (8 oz) shredded Swiss cheese
1 container (8 oz) reduced-fat sour cream

Frozen Foods
2 pkg (10-oz size) frozen lima beans
2 pkg (10-oz size) frozen corn
1 box (17 oz) frozen puff pastry

Bread
Dinner rolls (enough for Thanksgiving dinner)
1 loaf rye or whole-wheat bread, sliced

Basic Staples
Olive oil
Prepared salad dressing
Light brown sugar
Prepared orange juice
Ground nutmeg
Dried bay leaf
Salt and black pepper
Aluminum foil, large resealable plastic bags, plastic wrap

GAME PLAN

- To make life easier, here's our plan-ahead guide for your Thanksgiving dinner. Follow the "Turkey Day" list to assure correct timing for cooking dishes.

- Detailed storing and reheating tips follow each recipe.

- Recipes for gravy, cranberry sauce, salad, and desserts are not included, so be sure to add them to your plan.

- Although the recipe makes a generous amount of stuffing, the 7-day plan doesn't call for any leftovers, so don't deny your guests seconds—or thirds.

One Day Ahead

- Assemble leek stuffing.

- Precook succotash.

Turkey Day

- Bring turkey, stuffing, and succotash to room temperature.

- Start roasting turkey at 325°F.

- Start roasting potatoes at 325°F.

- Remove turkey from oven; increase oven temperature to 400°F, leave potatoes in and start cooking stuffing and squash.

- Warm succotash.

- Peel and mash potatoes.

- Toss salad.

Thanksgiving Dinner: Roast Turkey, Leek and Herbed Bread Stuffing, Confetti Succotash, Butternut Squash, Sour Cream Mashed Potatoes

────── SERVES 8 ──────

COOKING TIP

Start baking potatoes while turkey roasts—fit them in around the roasting pan. Finish baking potatoes, and cook stuffing and squash after turkey comes out, while turkey rests. Mash potatoes and warm succotash just before serving. We've not included a recipe for gravy—either make your own or use your favorite jarred brand.

Classic Roast Turkey

Here are the basic, no-fail directions from the National Turkey Federation for stuffing and cooking a frozen turkey. We used a 16-lb turkey to feed 8 people, with plenty of leftovers.

1. Thaw turkey. Remove giblets and neck from body and neck cavities. (To remove neck, it may be necessary to release legs from band of skin or the "hocklock," that metal or plastic legs-holder.) Rinse turkey inside and out with cool water, then pat dry with a paper towel.

2. If stuffing turkey, spoon prepared dressing loosely into body and neck cavities of turkey. Do not stuff turkey until just prior to roasting.

3. Return legs to hocklock or band of skin, or tie legs loosely with kitchen twine.

4. Place turkey, breast side up, on flat rack in shallow (2 inches deep) roasting pan. Brush turkey skin with oil or melted butter to prevent drying and promote browning.

5. Roast turkey in preheated 325°F oven on lowest oven rack (see chart below for approximate roasting times). When skin of turkey is golden brown, shield breast loosely with a rectangular piece of foil to prevent overbrowning. Turkey is done when an instant-read meat thermometer inserted in thickest part of thigh measures 180°F and drumstick is soft and moves easily at the joint. Stuffing should reach an internal temperature of 160°F.

6. Allow turkey to rest for 20 minutes before removing stuffing and carving.

208 | The *Working Mother* Cookbook

ROASTING TIMES
(325°F oven)

Weight	Unstuffed	Stuffed
8–12 lb	2¾–3 hr	3–3½ hr
12–14 lb	3–3¾ hr	3½–4 hr
14–18 lb	3¾–4¼ hr	4–4¼ hr
18–20 lb	4¼–4½ hr	4¼–4¾ hr
20–24 lb	4½–5 hr	4¾–5¼ hr

Leek-and-Herb Bread Stuffing

1 lb sliced bacon
4 T (½ stick) unsalted butter
4 celery stalks, sliced
1 bunch leeks, thinly sliced and rinsed (about 4)
½ tsp salt
½ tsp black pepper
1 pkg (12 oz–1 lb) packaged bread-stuffing mix (plain or seasoned)
1 cup walnuts, coarsely chopped
¼ cup fresh Italian parsley, chopped
1 T fresh thyme
1 T fresh sage, chopped
2–3 cups reduced-sodium chicken broth

1. In large Dutch oven or extra-large skillet over medium heat, cook bacon 6 minutes, or until just crisp. Drain on paper towels; crumble. Reserve ½ of bacon bits (about 1 cup) for later use. Pour off all but 2 T of the fat.

2. In same skillet over medium-low heat, melt 2 T of the butter in drippings; add celery, leeks, salt, and pepper. Cook 10 minutes, stirring. Transfer to a large bowl. Remove 1½ cups of mixture; reserve for later use. To vegetables remaining in skillet, stir in bacon, bread stuffing, walnuts, and all herbs. Gradually stir in broth, tossing gently to moisten evenly. (Use the full amount of broth if you are not stuffing the turkey.)

3. If not stuffing turkey: Place mixture in greased, large, shallow baking dish or roasting pan. Dot with remaining 2 T butter. Bake in preheated 400°F oven for 35 minutes, or until warmed through and lightly browned.

4. To stuff turkey: Let mixture cool completely after step 1, then loosely stuff turkey. Do not add remaining 2 T butter. Place any remaining stuffing in separate greased baking pan and bake as directed in step 3.

MAKE-AHEAD TIP

- *Prepare stuffing one day ahead through step 1.*
- *Cool, cover, and refrigerate.*
- *Remove from refrigerator 1 hour before continuing recipe.*
- *Dot with remaining 2 T butter; cover with foil and bake in 400°F oven for 20 minutes, then uncover and bake about 20 minutes longer. Or stuff as directed.*

Confetti Succotash

* *Prepare recipe one day ahead, omitting thyme, salt, and pepper.*
* *Cool, cover, and refrigerate.*
* *Remove from refrigerator 1 hour before continuing recipe. In covered saucepan over medium-high heat, cook about 10 minutes, or until hot, stirring occasionally. Stir in remaining ingredients.*
* *Reserve 4 cups for later use.*

If you make this recipe in advance, don't fully cook the veggies—the final warming will bring to desired consistency.

2 pkg (10-oz size) frozen lima beans, thawed
2 pkg (10-oz size) frozen corn kernels, thawed
1 lb fresh green beans, cut into 1-inch pieces
3 T unsalted butter
3 large shallots, chopped
2 T fresh thyme, or 1½ tsp dried
½ tsp salt
¼ tsp black pepper, optional

1. In Dutch oven or large saucepan over high heat, bring 4 cups water to a boil. Add lima beans; cook 2 minutes. Stir in corn and green beans. Cover and cook 5 minutes longer, or until beans are tender; drain.

2. Melt butter in same saucepan over medium-low heat; add shallots and cook 3 minutes, or until softened, stirring occasionally. Add cooked vegetables, thyme, salt, and pepper; heat through.

3. Reserve 4 cups for later use. Serve remaining succotash hot.

Brown-Sugar Butternut Squash

The best way to halve rock-hard squash: Using a heavy knife, slice off the stem. Stand squash on its end; cut down from top to bottom. These velvety vegetables are best served hot, so if there's not room in your oven to cook them while the turkey is still in, roast them while the turkey rests.

4 butternut squash (about 1¼ lb each)
2 T light-brown sugar
4 T (½ stick) unsalted butter, cut into 8 pieces
½ tsp salt
¼ tsp black pepper

1. Line a jelly roll or any low-sided baking pan with foil. Cut each squash in half; scoop out seeds. Arrange squash halves, cut-side up, in prepared pan. Sprinkle remaining ingredients over cut surfaces of squash.

2. Bake in preheated 400°F oven 15 minutes; turn cut-side down. Bake 20 minutes longer, or until tender.

3. Reserve 4 halves for later use.

4. Cut remaining halves in half vertically, to make 8 long wedges.

Sour-Cream Mashed Potatoes

10 *large russet potatoes (about 5½ lb)*
4 *T unsalted butter, cut into 4 pieces*
½ *cup whole milk*
½ *cup reduced-fat sour cream*
2 *T snipped fresh chives*
1 *tsp salt*
½ *tsp black pepper, optional*

1. Pierce skins of potatoes in several places with fork. Bake in 325°F oven with turkey for the last 1½ hours that the bird is in—then after you take the turkey out, leave the potatoes in and turn the oven up to 400°F for 30 minutes, or until very tender. Remove to cutting board.

2. When potatoes are cool enough to handle, peel 4 of the potatoes; place pulp in large bowl (discard peel).

3. Slice each of the remaining 6 potatoes into three slices lengthwise, each about ½-inch thick. We want to save the potato skins for later in the week.

4. Then peel skin off middle slice; place pulp in same large bowl (discard peel). With a spoon, scoop some of the pulp out of the 2 end pieces; add pulp to bowl. Leave a ¼-inch potato lining on the skins. Repeat process for each potato. You'll end up with 12 skins. Wrap them in plastic wrap and refrigerate for later use.

5. In small saucepan over low heat, melt butter in milk. In large saucepan over low heat, combine potato pulp and milk mixture. With potato masher or whisk, mash to desired consistency. Remove from heat.

6. Stir in remaining ingredients and serve hot.

TIMESAVING STRATEGIES

- Refrigerate 2¾ lb turkey meat to use Friday, Saturday, and Sunday.

- Refrigerate reserved 4 cups succotash to use Sunday.

- When reserved squash is cool, scoop out pulp (about 3 cups) and refrigerate, tightly covered, to use Friday.

- Refrigerate ½ cup prepared cranberry sauce to use Friday and Monday.

- Refrigerate reserved crumbled bacon (about 1 cup) in recloseable plastic bag to use Saturday and Monday.

- Refrigerate remaining 2 stalks celery to use Sunday.

- Refrigerate reserved 12 potato skin halves, tightly covered, to use Saturday.

Nutritional Information

PER SERVING TURKEY: 236 cal, 32 g protein, 11 g fat, 0 g carbohydrate, 93 mg cholesterol, 77 mg sodium

PER SERVING STUFFING: 305 cal, 8 g protein, 14 g fat, 38 g carbohydrate, 9 mg cholesterol, 781 mg sodium

PER SERVING SUCCOTASH: 138 cal, 5 g protein, 4 g fat, 24 g carbohydrate, 8 mg cholesterol, 113 mg sodium

PER SERVING SQUASH: 75 cal, 1 g protein, 3 g fat, 13 g carbohydrate, 8 mg cholesterol, 72 mg sodium

PER SERVING MASHED POTATOES: 332 cal, 6 g protein, 8 g fat, 61 g carbohydrate, 20 mg cholesterol, 272 mg sodium

Lazy Leftover Sandwiches

Everyone expects turkey sandwiches for dinner on the day after Thanksgiving. Here's a twist on the old favorite. And don't hesitate to add whatever you'd like—mayonnaise, leftover stuffing, lettuce.

8 slices rye or whole-wheat bread
12 oz roast turkey (reserved from Thursday), thinly sliced
½–1 cup shredded Swiss cheese
½ cup cranberry sauce (reserved from Thursday)

Preheat oven to 400°F. Make a sandwich with turkey slices, cheese, and sauce. Wrap each sandwich in foil; warm 15 minutes, until cheese melts.

Autumn Squash Soup

Bring squash to room temperature before making soup if possible—if not, cook the soup a little longer.

1 can (15 oz) solid-pack pumpkin
3 cups butternut squash pulp (reserved from Thursday)
1 tsp salt
¼ tsp black pepper
2 scallions, thinly sliced, optional garnish

1. In blender or food processor fitted with metal blade, combine first 2 ingredients and 2 cups water; puree until smooth. Reserve 1½ cups for later use.

2. In medium saucepan over medium-low heat, combine remaining puree, salt, pepper, and 2 cups water to desired consistency. Heat about 8 minutes, until warmed through. Garnish servings with scallions, if desired.

 TIMESAVING STRATEGIES

- Refrigerate ¼ cup cranberry sauce to use Monday.

- Refrigerate reserved 1½ cups squash soup, tightly covered, to use Tuesday.

Nutritional Information

PER SERVING OF SANDWICH: 419 cal, 36 g protein, 11 g fat, 46 g carbohydrate, 77 mg cholesterol, 473 mg sodium

PER SERVING OF SOUP: 64 cal, 2 g protein, 16 g fat, 0 g carbohydrate, 0 mg cholesterol, 274 mg sodium

Loaded Potato Skins

Serve these with a green salad. While you're getting this meal ready, prepare and freeze turkey-pie filling for a future meal (recipe pg. 217).

2 T unsalted butter
12 potato skin halves (reserved from Thursday)
½ cup low-fat sour cream
1 T snipped fresh chives
1 bag (8 oz) shredded cheddar cheese
½ cup cooked crumbled bacon (reserved from Thursday)

1. Preheat broiler. Melt butter. Place skins, cut-side up, on ungreased baking sheet. Brush surface of each potato skin, inside and out, with melted butter.

2. Broil 6 to 8 minutes, or until edges start to turn dark brown. Meanwhile, in small bowl, combine sour cream and chives.

3. Remove skins from oven. Sprinkle with cheese, then crumbled bacon. Broil 2 more minutes or until cheese is thoroughly melted. Serve hot, with sour cream mixture for dipping.

 TIMESAVING STRATEGIES

* Assemble turkey pie (recipe follows); cover and freeze for a future night.

* Reserve ½ cup crumbled bacon to use Monday.

Nutritional Information

PER SERVING: 544 cal, 22 g protein, 33 g fat, 42 g carbohydrate, 93 mg cholesterol, 542 mg sodium

Future Dinner: Puff-Pastry Turkey Pie

You make the filling for the turkey pie now; finish the recipe off on Monday. (See page 222.)

1 lb roast turkey (reserved from Thursday)
4 cups succotash (reserved from Thursday)
1 jar (10–12 oz) turkey gravy (or leftover)
1 tsp fresh thyme leaves or ½ tsp dried
½ tsp salt, optional

1. Cut turkey into ½-inch thick chunks. In large bowl, combine succotash, gravy, and thyme. Stir in turkey chunks until coated. Taste for seasoning; add salt and additional thyme, if desired.

2. Pour mixture into 9- by 9-inch baking pan or 10-inch pie plate. Cover pan with plastic, then foil; freeze for later use.

COOKING TIP

Taste the mixture before adding salt—the amount needed will depend on the saltiness of gravy.

Wild Rice and Turkey Salad with Cranberries

This recipe makes a lot—use leftovers for back-to-work lunches. To begin, thaw the pastry dough and prep the rolls for the oven, then start cooking the rice.

2 pkg (8-oz size) wild rice blend
9 oz roast turkey or about 2 cups pieces (reserved from Thursday)
2 stalks celery, diced
3 scallions, thinly sliced
½ cup walnuts, coarsely chopped
¼ cup cranberry sauce (reserved from Thursday)
¼ cup prepared balsamic vinegar dressing
3 T orange juice
2 T fresh Italian parsley, chopped
1 tsp salt
¼ tsp black pepper

1. Bring large pot of salted water to a boil over high heat. Add rice; cook like pasta about 16 minutes, until tender but not mushy. Drain and rinse. Reserve 3½ cups for later use.

2. Meanwhile, cut turkey into ½-inch chunks. In large serving bowl, combine cooked rice, turkey, celery, scallions, walnuts, and cranberry sauce. In small bowl, combine salad dressing, orange juice, parsley, salt, and pepper. Pour over salad; toss to mix. Let stand 20 minutes to blend flavors. Serve warm or at room temperature.

Swiss Cheese Rolls

½ pkg (17-oz size), or 1 sheet frozen puff pastry
1 cup shredded Swiss cheese

1. Thaw puff pastry for 30 minutes at room temperature. Preheat oven to 375°F.

2. When thawed, unfold pastry on lightly floured surface. Do not separate sections. Cut 9 squares from sheet, 3 per section. Keep remaining puff pastry sheet frozen for a future night.

3. Place squares on ungreased baking sheet; bake 12 minutes. Remove from oven.

4. Sprinkle rolls with 1 cup shredded Swiss cheese. Return to oven for 2 minutes, or until cheese melts and rolls are golden.

TIMESAVING STRATEGIES

- Prepare Turkey and Wild Rice Soup (recipe follows); freeze for a future night.
- Keep remaining puff pastry sheet frozen for a future night.

Nutritional Information

PER SERVING OF SALAD: 233 cal, 15 g protein, 13 g fat, 15 g carbohydrate, 32 mg cholesterol, 480 mg sodium
PER SERVING OF ROLLS: 261 cal, 7 g protein, 18 g fat, 18 g carbohydrate, 12 mg cholesterol, 131 mg sodium

Future Dinner: Turkey and Wild Rice Soup

This makes 9 cups of soup, enough for a meal for a family of 4—plus extra. If you prefer, freeze in smaller containers for single servings.

3½ cups cooked wild rice blend (reserved from above)
12 oz roast turkey (reserved from Thursday), cut into thin strips
1½ cups vegetable mixture (reserved from Thursday)
1 bay leaf
1 T fresh thyme
3 cans (13¾-oz size) reduced-sodium chicken broth
2 T chopped fresh Italian parsley
Pinch black pepper

1. In large Dutch oven over medium-high heat, combine first 5 ingredients; stir to coat.

2. Add broth; increase heat to high and bring just to a boil. Reduce heat and simmer 5 minutes to blend flavors.

3. Stir in pepper, parsley, and additional salt, if desired. Cool; pour into plastic containers and freeze for later use.

Nutritional Information

PER SERVING SOUP: 256 cal, 22 g protein, 8 g fat, 24 g carbohydrate, 54 mg cholesterol, 190 mg sodium

Pumpkin-Walnut Rigatoni

This dish is chock-full of vitamins and minerals, but most important, it's fast and delicious!

1 box (16 oz) rigatoni
1½ cups squash soup (reserved from Friday)
¼ cup whole milk
½ cup chopped walnuts
2 tsp chopped fresh sage or ½ tsp dried
½ tsp salt
⅛ tsp ground nutmeg

1. Cook rigatoni according to package directions; drain.

2. Meanwhile, in medium saucepan over low heat, combine soup, milk, walnuts, salt, and nutmeg (reserve a few walnuts to sprinkle on top). Stir to blend well and cook 2 minutes, to heat thoroughly.

3. In large serving bowl, toss drained pasta with sauce. Sprinkle with reserved walnuts.

Spinach Salad with Bacon Bits

Toss 1 bag (8 oz) baby spinach leaves with favorite prepared dressing and remaining ½ cup bacon bits.

Nutritional Information

PER SERVINGPASTA: 298 cal, 9 g protein, 11 g fat, 44 g carbohydrate, 2 mg cholesterol, 416 mg sodium
PER SERVING: salad: 117 cal, 4 g protein, 10 g fat, 4 g carbohydrate, 5 mg cholesterol, 362 mg sodium

Future Dinner: Puff-Pastry Turkey Pie

You've already made and frozen the filling. Now it's time to assemble the pie. You can keep it in your freezer for at least a month. When you want to serve it, defrost pie overnight in refrigerator, then allow to come to room temperature before baking. We like this served with a green salad. It should feed four.

½ pkg (17-oz size) frozen puff pastry (1 sheet)
Turkey-pie filling (reserved from Saturday)

1. Preheat oven to 375°F. Thaw pastry sheet according to package directions. Unfold sheet on lightly floured surface; cut out a 10½-inch circle.

2. Dampen the rim of a 10-inch pie plate with water. Fill plate with turkey mixture; top with pastry and crimp edges.

3. Cut 4 slashes in pastry; decorate with scraps. Place pie plate on a baking sheet; bake 35 to 40 minutes, until golden brown.

Nutritional Information

PER SERVING: 683 cal, 45 g protein, 33 g fat, 53 g carbohydrate, 95 mg cholesterol, 745 mg sodium

Desserts: Sweet and Simple

• • •

How the Desserts are Organized

Desserts don't have to be complicated or fancy to delight. You'll find these sweet ideas simple, yet wholly satisfying. If dessert is served in your home, most days it consists of cookies out of a bag or ice cream from the carton. For those days, we've come up with some 5-Minute Marvels.

Sometimes, however, it's fun to present something just a little special—for a family celebration, or if you want to bake with the kids. For those days, make one of our fruit tarts—they're easy to put together, but do require a little baking time. If you're expecting guests, try our fabulous Petal Phyllo Cream Cups. (See photo.)

Three Tasty Tarts

•   •   •

Puff-Pastry Tart

Frozen puff pastry is one of those convenience products that is quite high in quality. It's available in sheets, for full-size tarts, or molded shells. This recipe makes one large, rustic, free-form tart, but you could also pour this filling into shells for individual treats. You may substitute apples, peaches, or plums, depending on what's in season. The pastry will keep in your freezer for months—just make sure to use an all-butter variety.

1 sheet (½ of a 17-oz pkg) frozen puff pastry
3 large ripe pears
1 large egg
¼ cup granulated sugar
Pinch nutmeg
2 T milk

1. Thaw pastry as directed. Preheat oven to 325°F. Meanwhile, peel pears and slice into ½-inch-thick wedges. In medium bowl, toss pears with egg, sugar, and nutmeg.

2. Open pastry sheet and lay on ungreased baking sheet. With your palms, flatten out seams in pastry. Spread pear mixture over pastry, leaving a 1-inch border around sides.

3. Pull up the edges of pastry, gently stretching to partially cover filling. With a pastry brush or your fingers, brush the exposed crust with milk. Bake 30 minutes, until filling is bubbly and crust is golden brown.

Oatmeal-Apple Crumble

This is the one pie crust recipe we couldn't live without. It's incredibly tasty—you'll be tempted to eat it all up before you even make the pie. (To tell the truth, there have been times we've doubled the recipe, just so everyone could eat some of the dough!) It's also endlessly flexible; it doesn't need to be rolled out; it works with any fruit or berry (adjust sugar and baking times, if needed); and it can be made in advance. Keep crumble mixture tightly covered in refrigerator up to 3 days. To freeze, press mixture into pie tin, press plastic wrap firmly to surface, then wrap in foil and freeze up to 1 month.

½ cup (1 stick) unsalted butter
1 cup all-purpose flour
1 cup old-fashioned oatmeal
½ cup granulated sugar
¼ tsp salt
6 tart apples, such as Granny Smith
¼ tsp ground cinnamon

1. Preheat oven to 400°F. In small saucepan over low heat, melt butter. In large bowl, combine flour, oatmeal, sugar, and salt. Add melted butter, stir to combine. Press ¾ of mixture into 9-inch pie tin.

2. Peel and thinly slice apples. In large bowl, combine apple slices with remaining ingredients. Evenly spread over crust in pan. Sprinkle with remaining crumbs. Bake 40 minutes, until fruit is bubbly.

Quick Fruit Crisp

This recipe makes enough for a light topping for an 8- or 9-inch pie; double the crust if you want a thicker top crust or to add a bottom crust. (You'll need two cans of fruit for a 9-inch pie.) Here's a recipe that's perfect for baking with kids—little hands are just right for sprinkling the topping over the fruit.

1 cup all-purpose flour
¼ cup granulated sugar
⅛ tsp salt
½ cup (1 stick) unsalted butter, cold and cut into 8 pieces
1 can (21 oz) pie filling or 6 cups sliced fruit mixed with ½ cup granulated sugar

1. Preheat oven to 400°F. In large bowl of electric mixer on medium speed, mix first 3 ingredients for 10 seconds. Add butter pieces; mix for 1 minute, until mixture forms big, loose crumbs.

2. Pour fruit into 8-inch pie tin. Sprinkle crumbs evenly over fruit. Place pie on baking sheet (to catch any drips) and bake 30 to 40 minutes, until topping is golden brown and fruit bubbly.

Chocolate for Every Occasion

•   •   •

Chocolate Ganache

Here's an all-purpose chocolate sensation. It takes minutes to assemble, yet has tons of uses. If used warm, it's a chocolate sauce. If cooled until slightly thickened, it's a shiny glaze for a 9-inch cake. When refrigerated, it becomes a thick, fudgy filling for cookie sandwiches. If chilled, then whipped, it's enough frosting for a 9-inch cake. You can even make it 2 days in advance; store, tightly wrapped in the refrigerator.

1 carton (8 oz) heavy cream
1 T unsalted butter
8 oz bittersweet or semisweet chocolate, coarsely chopped

1. In small saucepan over medium-low heat, warm cream and butter until butter melts and tiny bubbles appear around edge of pot. Do not boil.

2. Meanwhile, place chocolate pieces in medium bowl. Pour cream over chocolate. Cover bowl with plastic wrap and let sit 8 minutes. Stir until completely blended and shiny. (Be patient, this takes a few minutes.) At this point, ganache may be used as a sauce. Refrigerate 10 minutes, until thickened, to use as a glaze.

3. For frosting: Refrigerate 45 minutes, then, with wooden spoon or electric mixer, beat until thick and creamy and of desired consistency. Do not overbeat, or it will become fudge. If it becomes too thick, stir in 1 T warm heavy cream.

One Showstopper

Petal Phyllo Cream Cups

Phyllo (filo) is a paper-thin pastry specialty of Greek bakers. When filo is layered with a little butter and baked, it becomes a magnificent flaky crust. Don't be put off by the steps involved; it's a snap once you get the hang of it. To prevent drying, it's important to cover the sheets with plastic wrap or foil when you aren't using them. After removing the sheets you need from the package, any leftover filo can be refrozen.

Butter-flavored cooking spray
4 sheets phyllo dough, thawed if frozen
2 T granulated sugar
Prepared whipped topping or vanilla yogurt
Mixed berries for garnish

1. Preheat oven to 375°F. Set oven rack in middle of oven. Coat 12-cup muffin tin with cooking spray.

2. Stack phyllo sheets flat on work surface. Using scissors, cut entire stack lengthwise in half, then crosswise into thirds. (You should have 6 stacks of sheets.) Cover squares with plastic or foil.

3. Gently peel off and press one of the squares into a muffin cup, pushing down to the edges of the cup. Coat lightly with cooking spray, reaching the entire sheet, including edges. Sprinkle sheet with sugar. Add a second sheet, rotated so that the corners do not line up; press into cup, then spray and sugar. Add a third sheet, again rotated, fitted in, then sprayed and sugared. Move on to another cup; repeat with remaining filo sheets, to fill 8 muffin cups. To prevent crust from puffing up when baking, crumple some foil into a ball and fill into cup.

4. Bake 8 minutes, until golden and crisp. Cool cups, still in tin, on wire rack. When ready to fill and serve, carefully lift cup onto serving plate; fill with whipped topping or vanilla yogurt; garnish with berries.

5-Minute Marvels

•   •   •

Six 5-Minute Marvels

The simplest ending to any meal is a sweet, ripe piece of seasonal fruit. But you may have a hard time convincing your kids that fruit is a treat. Hence, some speedy dessert ideas.

1. Fill prepared graham-cracker crusts with instant pudding, prepared lemon curd, Nutella, whipped cream, or any flavor yogurt; top with berries or crushed cookies. Or, create dessert sandwiches using graham-cracker squares or animal-shape cookies and one of above fillings.

2. Give a bowl of ice cream a boost by topping with fresh fruit in complementary flavors. For example, coconut ice cream with sliced mango, papaya, or kiwi fruit, or dark chocolate ice cream with fresh cherries.

3. In a stemmed glass, layer ice cream with crushed candies or cookies. Try vanilla layered with crushed peppermints, chocolate-covered peppermint patties, and topped with chocolate sauce. Or layer alternate sorbets (try lemon and raspberry) with crushed macaroons in between.

4. Turn a purchased pound cake on its side; cut lengthwise into 4 large slices. With a cookie cutter (use simple shapes, like hearts or stars), cut shapes from each slice. Sandwich whipped cream or softened ice cream and fresh berries between 2 shaped cake slices.

5. For a two-minute topping for cakes, sundaes, or fruit, combine 1 cup heavy cream with ½ cup chocolate syrup and 2 T confectioners' sugar, or ½ cup strawberry syrup; beat until mixture holds soft peaks. This fluffy creation is also great with individually prepared shortcakes and fresh berries.

6. Let the kids make their own fondue by combining 1½ cups chocolate syrup with ⅔ cup peanut butter. Serve with sliced fruit stuck on skewers for dipping.

Index

CREDITS
Food Editor: Susan Lilly Ott

Recipe Development:
Laurie Clearley
Susan Shapiro Jaslove
Helen Taylor Jones
Lori Longbotham
David Ott
Susan Lilly Ott
Julia Pemberton
Victoria Abbot Riccardi
Jodi Weatherstone
Diane Worthington

Food Testing:
Jodi Weatherstone

Photo Editor:
Martha Maristany

Photography:
Beatriz DaCosta; Seared salmon, Dijon pork chops, Pulled pork sandwich, Chorizo chili, Baked penne, Grill It-7 menu, New Family Favorites-7 day menu, Touch of the Tropics-7 day menu, Pennsylvania Dutch Treat-7 menu, Holiday Feasting-7 day menu, Petal phyllo

Mary Ellen Bartley; Corn tortilla soup, Meatball ABCs

Dana Gallagher; Mashed potato salad, Creamy pasta salad

Mark Ferri, Tuna Niçoise, Garlicky shrimp

Food Styling:
William Smith
Roscoe Betsill

Props:
Denise Canter
Martha Maristany

Book Development:
D&M Publishing for *Working Mother* Magazine

DATE DUE FOR RETURN

ROBERT LEPAGE
CONNECTING FLIGHTS

ROBERT LEPAGE CONNECTING FLIGHTS

RÉMY CHAREST

Translated from the French by Wanda Romer Taylor

METHUEN

Published by Methuen

First published as *Quelques zones de liberté* in 1995 by
Editions de L'instant même, Québec

Copyright © 1995 by Rémy Charest, Robert Lepage,
Editions de L'instant même, Ex Machina
Translation copyright © 1997 by Wanda Romer Taylor

Rémy Charest, Robert Lepage, Editions de L'instant même, Ex Machina
have asserted their rights under the Copyright, Designs and Patents Act, 1988
to be identified as the authors of this work.

Cover photograph by Bengt Wanselius
Other photographs by Véro Boncompagni, Michael Cooper, Armando Gallo, Claudel
Huot, François Lachapelle, Daniel Mallard, Emmanuel Valette, Bengt Wanselius
reproduced by kind permission

First published in the United Kingdom in 1997 by Methuen,
Random House, 20 Vauxhall Bridge Road, London SW1V 2SA

Random House Australia (Pty) Limited
20 Alfred Street, Milsons Point, Sydney,
New South Wales 2061, Australia

Random House New Zealand Limited
18 Poland Road, Glenfield
Auckland 10, New Zealand

Random House South Africa (Pty) Limited
Endulini, 5A Jubilee Road, Parktown 2193, South Africa

Random House UK Limited Reg. No. 954009

A CIP catalogue rocord for this book
is available fom the British Library

ISBN 0413 70690 7

Typeset in Bembo by MATS, Southend-on-Sea, Essex
Printed and bound in Great Britain by Mackays of Chatham PLC